TENNESSEE BUCKET LIST

George B. Gilson

Tennessee Bucket List Guide

Embark on 100 thrilling expeditions: Discover the most exclusive hidden attractions and essential destinations to fulfill your aspirations and make enduring memories.

(Map included.)

George B. Gilson

If you enjoyed exploring Tennessee with this book, would you please consider writing an honest review?

REFER TO MAPS SECTION TO VIEW THE INTERACTIVE MAPS

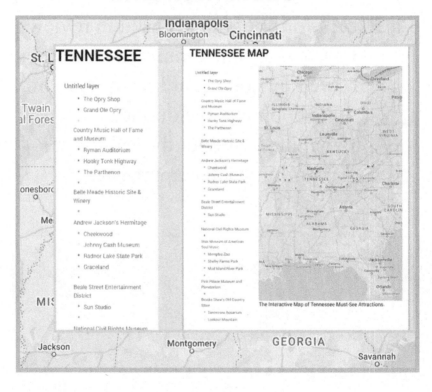

Table of Contents

INTRODUCTION

Tennessee, a state known for its rich musical heritage, stunning natural beauty, and warm Southern hospitality, is a must-visit destination for anyone seeking a diverse and memorable travel experience. The "Tennessee Bucket List Guide" is your essential companion to discovering the unique gems, must-see sites, and offbeat destinations that make this state a true gem in the heart of the South.

Imagine strolling through the vibrant streets of Nashville, known as the "Music City," where you can immerse yourself in the sounds of country, rock, and blues at iconic venues like the Grand Ole Opry and the Ryman Auditorium. Picture yourself exploring the majestic Great Smoky Mountains National Park, where you can hike through lush forests, spot wildlife, and take in breathtaking views of cascading waterfalls and rolling hills.

This guide will take you through all the remarkable sites across Tennessee's varied landscapes, from the bustling cities and charming small towns to the serene lakes and rugged wilderness areas. Whether you're fascinated by history, captivated by nature, or drawn to cultural experiences, this guide covers it all. Each destination is carefully selected and described in detail, with practical information including addresses and GPS coordinates to ensure you can easily find your way.

We've also included tips on the best times to visit each location, helping you plan your journey to experience each place at its finest. From exploring the historical significance of the Hermitage, the home of President Andrew Jackson, to enjoying the vibrant festivals like the

Bonnaroo Music and Arts Festival, there's something for everyone.

Discover interesting facts about each destination, and stay informed with links to their official websites. Learn about the rich musical heritage at the Country Music Hall of Fame and Museum, or experience the lively atmosphere at the Beale Street Music Festival in Memphis.

Welcome to Tennessee, where every visit is a new adventure. Whether you're soaking in the rich history, indulging in the delicious Southern cuisine, or simply enjoying the great outdoors, Tennessee offers an enriching and memorable experience. Let the "Tennessee Bucket List Guide" be your trusted companion as you explore the heart and soul of this remarkable state. Welcome to Tennessee, where your next great adventure begins.

Tennessee's Rich History and Culture

Tennessee is a state full of history and culture, offering a mix of Native American heritage, colonial history, and a lively arts scene. This guide explores the unique features that shape Tennessee, from its early days to its modern cultural landscape.

Native American Heritage: Before European settlers arrived, Tennessee was home to many Native American tribes, including the Cherokee and Chickasaw. These tribes had rich cultures and communities that thrived on the land's resources. Today, you can learn about their history at various museums and historical sites across the state.

Colonial and Revolutionary Era: Tennessee was part of the early American colonies and became a place of refuge for many seeking freedom. The state played an important role during the American Revolution, with its residents actively participating in the fight for independence. Historic sites like the Andrew Jackson's Hermitage and Fort Donelson showcase Tennessee's contributions to the nation's founding.

Maritime Tradition: Tennessee's rivers and lakes have been vital to its growth, supporting a strong tradition of boating and fishing. The Tennessee River and the Great Smoky Mountains National Park are popular for outdoor activities and celebrate the state's connection to water and nature.

The Industrial Revolution: During the Industrial Revolution, Tennessee saw significant growth, especially in cities like Nashville and Memphis. Factories and railroads transformed the economy, attracting many immigrants who added to the state's rich cultural mix. The history of this period can be explored at various museums, including the Tennessee State Museum.

The Gilded Age: In the late 19th century, Tennessee experienced a time of great wealth, especially in Nashville. The city's grand homes and buildings reflect this era of prosperity. Many of these historic sites are open to the public, allowing visitors to glimpse life during this opulent time.

Civil Rights and Social Progress: Tennessee has a strong history of social movements, including the fight for civil rights. The state was a key location for many important events in the civil rights movement, and today, it continues to promote equality and justice through various initiatives and programs.

Arts and Culture: Today, Tennessee is known for its vibrant arts scene, particularly in Nashville and Memphis. Nashville, often called "Music City," is famous for its country music, while Memphis is known for blues and rock 'n' roll. The state hosts numerous music festivals and cultural events, showcasing its artistic spirit.

Tennessee's food scene is also diverse, blending traditional Southern cuisine with flavors from various cultures. From barbecue to hot chicken, the state's culinary offerings reflect its rich history and cultural diversity.

Festivals and Events: Tennessee hosts many festivals celebrating music, food, and culture. Events like the Bonnaroo Music and Arts Festival and the Memphis in May International Festival attract visitors from around the world, highlighting the state's lively community spirit.

An Ever-Evolving Legacy: Tennessee's history and culture are always changing, blending its rich past with modern influences. The state offers visitors a chance to experience a place where history is alive. Whether exploring historic sites, enjoying beautiful landscapes, or participating in local events, Tennessee provides a unique mix of old and new, making it a fascinating destination for everyone.

How to Use This Guide

Welcome to your comprehensive guide for exploring the rich history, diverse culture, and natural beauty of Tennessee. This book is designed to be your ultimate companion, highlighting must-see places while providing practical information to ensure your journey is smooth and enjoyable.

Guide Organization

This guide is organized into detailed sections, each focusing on a unique aspect of Tennessee:

Historical Landmarks: Discover Tennessee's rich heritage by visiting iconic sites such as the Hermitage, the Parthenon in Nashville, and the National Civil Rights Museum in Memphis. These locations offer insights into the stories and architecture that have shaped the state.

Natural Attractions: Explore Tennessee's stunning landscapes, including its parks, mountains, and rivers. From the trails of Great Smoky Mountains National Park to the lakes of the Tennessee Valley, these destinations showcase the state's diverse ecosystems.

Cultural Events: Engage with Tennessee's vibrant cultural scene by attending festivals, performances, and local traditions. Enjoy events like the Bonnaroo Music and Arts Festival, the Memphis in May celebration, and the Nashville Film Festival.

Each section includes a description of the location, key highlights, directions, and practical tips on what to bring to enhance your visit.

GPS Coordinates and Directions

To make navigation easy, each destination includes precise GPS coordinates. You can enter these into Google Maps for straightforward navigation. For locations without a physical address, GPS coordinates ensure you can find your way effortlessly.

Interactive Map and QR Code

Enhance your travel planning with an interactive map accessible via a QR code or provided link. This digital map includes:

Interactive Map: A comprehensive display of all featured destinations in this guide. It helps you visualize your journey, plan routes, and discover nearby attractions, ensuring you make the most of your trip.

Tips for a Smooth Journey

Preparation: Some areas in Tennessee may have limited cell signal. It's advisable to download maps and directions for offline use before setting out.

Backup Power: Consider bringing a portable charger for your devices to stay connected and capture memories.

Seasonal Insights: Each destination includes information on the best times to visit, helping you plan your trip to coincide with ideal weather conditions and seasonal events.

Cost Information: This guide provides details on any entry fees, permits, or costs associated with each destination, allowing you to budget effectively and avoid surprises.

Making the Most of Your Adventure

This guide is more than just a list of places to visit; it's an invitation to immerse yourself in the unique charm and allure of Tennessee. Whether you're exploring historical landmarks, savoring local cuisine, or enjoying the arts, each destination offers an opportunity to create unforgettable memories.

Happy travels, and enjoy the many wonders that Tennessee has to offer!

Landscape of Tennessee

Tennessee is known for its beautiful and varied landscapes, featuring majestic mountains, rolling hills, winding rivers, and charming rural areas. Despite its size, the state offers a rich variety of natural scenery that attracts visitors from near and far.

Mountain Beauty

Tennessee's mountains are one of its most defining features. The Great Smoky Mountains National Park is famous for its stunning views, diverse wildlife, and beautiful hiking trails. The park is a popular destination for outdoor activities like hiking, camping, and wildlife watching. Other mountain ranges, such as the Cumberland Plateau, provide breathtaking scenery and opportunities for adventure.

Lush Forests and Parks

The interior of Tennessee is home to lush forests and expansive state parks that offer outdoor enthusiasts plenty of recreational opportunities. Parks like Percy Warner Park and Radnor Lake State Park are popular for hiking, picnicking, and birdwatching, providing a peaceful escape from city life. The Land Between the Lakes National Recreation Area offers trails for hiking, biking, and fishing, as well as beautiful lakes for boating.

Serene Rivers and Waterways

Tennessee's rivers, such as the Tennessee River and the Cumberland River, play a crucial role in the state's ecosystem and history. The rivers provide opportunities for kayaking, canoeing, and fishing, allowing visitors to enjoy the state's natural beauty from a different perspective. The Tennessee River, in particular, is known for its scenic views and recreational activities.

Rolling Countryside and Rural Charm

The rural areas of Tennessee, especially in the west and middle parts of the state, feature rolling hills and farmland. These areas are dotted with charming small towns, historic homes, and scenic byways. The town of Franklin, with its historic downtown and beautiful landscapes, exemplifies the pastoral beauty of the region. Tennessee is also famous for its vibrant fall foliage, attracting many visitors each autumn.

Unique Natural Landmarks

Tennessee boasts several unique natural landmarks that offer visitors a chance to explore distinctive landscapes. The Ruby Falls in Chattanooga is a stunning underground waterfall, while the Great Smoky Mountains are home to Clingmans Dome, the highest point in the state. These landmarks provide opportunities for hiking, photography, and enjoying the great outdoors.

A Haven for Nature Enthusiasts

Tennessee's diverse landscapes provide a haven for nature lovers and outdoor adventurers. Whether you're drawn to the mountains, peaceful forests, or scenic rivers, Tennessee offers a wealth of natural beauty to explore and enjoy. The state's unique mix of mountainous and rural environments, along with its rich history and cultural attractions, makes it a remarkable destination for visitors seeking both relaxation and adventure.

Climate of Tennessee

Tennessee has a humid subtropical climate, which means it experiences four distinct seasons with different temperatures and levels of rainfall. The state's varied geography, including mountains and valleys, influences its climate, leading to differences in weather across the region.

Summer: Summers in Tennessee are typically warm and humid. In July, the hottest month, average high temperatures range from 85°F to 95°F (29°C to 35°C). Humidity can raise the temperature. Many people visit Tennessee during the summer to enjoy outdoor activities, music festivals, and the beautiful scenery. Thunderstorms are common in the afternoons, especially in July and August, bringing brief but heavy rain.

Winter: Winters in Tennessee can be cold, with average high temperatures in January, the coldest month, ranging from 40°F to 50°F (4°C to 10°C). The eastern part of the state, especially in the mountains, can experience more snowfall compared to the western regions. Snowfall varies but can average around 5 to 10 inches (13 to 25 cm) annually. In the west, it is more common to see rain than snow during winter storms.

Spring

Spring in Tennessee is a season of change, with warming temperatures and blooming flowers. Average high temperatures in March range from 55°F to 65°F (13°C to 18°C), increasing to 70°F to 80°F (21°C to 27°C) by May. This season also brings more rainfall, which helps the plants grow. Spring can sometimes be foggy, especially in the mornings.

Fall

Autumn is a beautiful time in Tennessee, with cooler temperatures and colorful leaves. Average high temperatures in September range from 75°F to 85°F (24°C to 29°C), dropping to 50°F to 60°F (10°C to 16°C) by November. Fall is popular for outdoor activities like hiking and enjoying the stunning fall foliage, especially in the Great Smoky Mountains.

Rainfall

Tennessee receives a good amount of rainfall throughout the year, with annual precipitation averaging around 50 to 60 inches (1,270 to 1,520 mm). Rain is fairly evenly spread out, but spring and fall can see more frequent showers. The state can also be affected by tropical storms and hurricanes, especially in late summer and early fall.

Extreme Weather

Tennessee can experience extreme weather events, including tornadoes, severe thunderstorms, and winter storms. The peak of tornado season is in the spring, while winter storms can bring snow and ice, especially in the higher elevations.

The diverse climate of Tennessee, with its distinct seasons, supports many outdoor activities and showcases the state's natural beauty year-round. Whether you're enjoying summer festivals, vibrant fall colors, snowy winter landscapes, or blooming spring gardens, Tennessee offers a welcoming environment for both visitors and residents.

Middle Tennessee

The Grand Ole Opry (Nashville)

Why You Should Visit: The Grand Ole Opry is a legendary live music venue that is considered the heart of country music. It hosts performances by country music legends and up-and-coming artists, offering a blend of history and entertainment. Visiting the Opry is a quintessential Nashville experience, capturing the essence of the genre's cultural significance.

Website: (https://www.opry.com/)

Location: 2804 Opryland Drive, Nashville, TN 37214

What to do: Attend live country music performances.

Packing list: Casual attire, camera, and light jacket.

Best Time to Visit: Year-round; check the schedule for special events.

Fees: Ticket prices vary; typically $40-$100.

How to Get There: Accessible by car, with ample parking; public transport options also available.

Closest Town for Accommodation: Gaylord Opryland Resort & Convention Center offers luxury accommodations with a water park and multiple dining options. Location: 2800 Opryland Drive, Nashville, TN 37214, Phone: (615) 889-1000.

GPS Coordinates: 36.2067° N, 86.6922° W

Interesting Facts: The Grand Ole Opry is the longest-running radio broadcast in U.S. history, starting in 1925.

Country Music Hall of Fame and Museum (Nashville)

Why You Should Visit: The Country Music Hall of Fame and Museum is a treasure trove of country music history, showcasing artifacts, exhibits, and memorabilia from the genre's biggest stars. It's an educational and entertaining experience that highlights the evolution and cultural impact of country music.

Website: (https://countrymusichalloffame.org/)

Location: 222 5th Ave S, Nashville, TN 37203

What to do: Explore interactive exhibits and view historic memorabilia.

Packing list: Comfortable walking shoes and a camera.

Best Time to Visit: Anytime; indoor venue suitable for all seasons.

Fees: General admission is approximately $25.

How to Get There: Located in downtown Nashville, accessible by car, bus, or walking.

Closest Town for Accommodation: Hilton Nashville Downtown offers spacious suites, dining options, and a fitness center. Location: 121 4th Ave S, Nashville, TN 37201, Phone: (615) 620-1000.

GPS Coordinates: 36.1580° N, 86.7774° W

Interesting Facts: The museum's architecture includes elements that symbolize a piano keyboard, reflecting its musical focus.

Ryman Auditorium (Nashville)

Why You Should Visit: Known as the "Mother Church of Country Music," the Ryman Auditorium is a historic venue with a rich legacy of hosting legendary performances. Its acoustics are renowned, making it a favorite among artists and audiences alike. The venue's history adds a layer of depth to its already impressive allure.

Website: (https://ryman.com/)

Location: 116 5th Ave N, Nashville, TN 37219

What to do: Attend concerts and take guided tours.

Packing list: Comfortable shoes and a camera.

Best Time to Visit: Year-round; check for concert schedules.

Fees: Tour tickets are around $25; concert ticket prices vary.

How to Get There: Centrally located in downtown Nashville, accessible by car, bus, or walking.

Closest Town for Accommodation: Renaissance Nashville Hotel offers modern accommodations with dining and a fitness center. Location: 611 Commerce St, Nashville, TN 37203, Phone: (615) 255-8400.

GPS Coordinates: 36.1616° N, 86.7785° W

Interesting Facts: The Ryman was originally built as a church in 1892 and became the home of the Grand Ole Opry from 1943 to 1974.

Broadway Honky-Tonks (Nashville)

Why You Should Visit: Broadway in Nashville is famous for its vibrant nightlife and honky-tonk bars, where live music plays daily. It's the heartbeat of Nashville's entertainment scene, offering a lively atmosphere and a taste of Southern culture.

Website: (https://www.visitmusiccity.com/things-to-do-nightlife)

Location: Broadway, Nashville, TN 37203

What to do: Enjoy live music, dancing, and local cuisine.

Packing list: Casual attire, ID for entry, and comfortable shoes.

Best Time to Visit: Evenings and weekends for the best nightlife experience.

Fees: Generally, no cover charge; food and drink prices vary.

How to Get There: Easily accessible by foot, car, or public transport.

Closest Town for Accommodation: Hyatt Centric Downtown Nashville offers modern amenities, a rooftop bar, and city views. Location: 210 3rd Ave S, Nashville, TN 37201, Phone: (615) 255-4987.

GPS Coordinates: 36.1628° N, 86.7816° W

Interesting Facts: Broadway is known as the "Honky Tonk Highway," where many famous musicians, including Willie Nelson and Kris Kristofferson, began their careers.

The Parthenon (Nashville)

Why You Should Visit: The Parthenon in Nashville is a full-scale replica of the ancient Parthenon in Athens, Greece. It serves as an art museum and a symbol of Nashville's cultural heritage as the "Athens of the South." The structure also features the tallest indoor statue in the Western world, Athena Parthenos.

Website:(https://www.nashville.gov/departments/parks/parthenon)

Location: 2500 West End Ave, Nashville, TN 37203

What to do: Explore the art museum and admire the architecture.

Packing list: Comfortable walking shoes and a camera.

Best Time to Visit: For mild temperatures, spring and fall.

Fees: Admission is around $10.

How to Get There: Located in Centennial Park, accessible by car or public transport.

Closest Town for Accommodation: Loews Vanderbilt Hotel offers upscale accommodations and dining. Location: 2100 West End Ave, Nashville, TN 37203, Phone: (615) 320-1700.

GPS Coordinates: 36.1497° N, 86.8133° W

Interesting Facts: The Parthenon was originally built for the Tennessee Centennial Exposition in 1897 and houses a 42-foot statue of Athena.

Belle Meade Plantation (Nashville)

Why You Should Visit: Belle Meade Plantation offers a glimpse into the Antebellum South with its historic mansion, winery, and beautiful grounds. Known for its horse breeding legacy, the plantation provides guided tours that delve into the lives of those who lived and worked there.

Website: (https://bellemeadeplantation.com/)

Location: 5025 Harding Pike, Nashville, TN 37205

What to do: Take guided tours, wine tasting, and explore the grounds.

Packing list: Comfortable shoes, sunscreen, and a camera.

Best Time to Visit: Spring and fall for pleasant weather and garden tours.

Fees: Admission is around $24.

How to Get There: Located west of downtown Nashville, accessible by car.

Closest Town for Accommodation: Hampton Inn & Suites Nashville-Green Hills offers modern amenities and easy access to shopping and dining. Location: 2324 Crestmoor Rd, Nashville, TN 37215, Phone: (615) 777-0001.

GPS Coordinates: 36.1073° N, 86.8692° W

Interesting Facts: Belle Meade was famous for breeding thoroughbred horses, including Iroquois, the first American-bred horse to win the English Derby.

The Hermitage (Nashville)

Why You Should Visit: The Hermitage is the historical home of Andrew Jackson, the 7th President of the United States. The site offers an immersive experience into the life and times of Jackson and early American history, with well-preserved buildings, gardens, and artifacts.

Website: (https://thehermitage.com/)

Location: 4580 Rachels Ln, Hermitage, TN 37076

What to do: Explore the mansion, gardens, and museum exhibits.

Packing list: Comfortable shoes, camera, and weather-appropriate clothing.

Best Time to Visit: Spring and fall for the best weather and garden views.

Fees: Admission is around $20.

How to Get There: Located 20 minutes east of downtown Nashville by car.

Closest Town for Accommodation: Holiday Inn Express & Suites Nashville-Opryland offers comfortable rooms, complimentary breakfast, and a fitness center. Location: 2461 McGavock Pk, Nashville, TN 37214, Phone: (615) 823-6000.

GPS Coordinates: 36.2151° N, 86.6120° W

Interesting Facts: The Hermitage includes Jackson's tomb and a museum with exhibits on his life and presidency.

Cheekwood Estate & Gardens (Nashville)

Why You Should Visit: Cheekwood Estate & Gardens is a stunning 55-acre estate featuring a botanical garden and an art museum. It is known for its beautiful seasonal displays, including blooming tulips in spring and Christmas lights during the holidays. The estate also offers a rich cultural experience with rotating art exhibits and sculptures.

Website: (https://cheekwood.org)

Location: 1200 Forrest Park Dr, Nashville, TN 37205

What to do: Explore themed gardens, art exhibits, and seasonal festivals.

Packing list: Comfortable walking shoes, camera, and weather-appropriate attire.

Best Time to Visit: Spring and fall for the best garden displays and weather.

Fees: $20 to $25, depending on the season and events.

How to Get There: Accessible by car with parking available; public transit options are also nearby.

Closest Town for Accommodation: Loews Vanderbilt Hotel offers upscale accommodations with amenities like a fitness center and on-site dining. Location: 2100 West End Ave, Nashville, TN 37203, Phone: (615) 320-1700.

GPS Coordinates: 36.0895° N, 86.8705° W

Interesting Facts: The estate was originally the residence of the Cheek family, who made their fortune from Maxwell House Coffee. It was opened to the public in 1960 as a museum and garden.

Johnny Cash Museum (Nashville)

Why You Should Visit: The Johnny Cash Museum is dedicated to the life and music of the legendary "Man in Black." It features the most comprehensive collection of Johnny Cash artifacts and memorabilia, including handwritten lyrics, stage costumes, and instruments. The museum provides an intimate look at Cash's career and his impact on music and culture.

Website: (https://www.johnnycashmuseum.com)

Location: 119 3rd Ave S, Nashville, TN 37201

What to do: Explore exhibits detailing Johnny Cash's life and music legacy.

Packing list: Casual attire, camera, and a fan of Johnny Cash's music.

Best Time to Visit: Open year-round; weekdays are less crowded.

Fees: General admission is around $22.

How to Get There: Located in downtown Nashville, easily accessible by car, foot, or public transport.

Closest Town for Accommodation: Renaissance Nashville Hotel offers modern rooms, dining options, and a central location near attractions. Location: 611 Commerce St, Nashville, TN 37203, Phone: (615) 255-8400.

GPS Coordinates: 36.1606° N, 86.7777° W

Interesting Facts: The museum also includes a section dedicated to June Carter Cash, showcasing their love story and collaborative work.

Radnor Lake State Park (Nashville)

Why You Should Visit: Radnor Lake State Park is a serene natural area known for its scenic beauty and diverse wildlife. It offers a peaceful retreat for nature lovers, with hiking trails, wildlife observation points, and picturesque lake views. The park is a haven for bird watchers and photographers, providing a natural escape close to the city.

Website: (https://tnstateparks.com/parks/radnor-lake)

Location: 1160 Otter Creek Rd, Nashville, TN 37220

What to do: Hiking, wildlife viewing, and photography.

Packing list: Hiking shoes, binoculars, water, and a camera.

Best Time to Visit: Spring and fall for pleasant temperatures and vibrant foliage.

Fees: No entrance fee.

How to Get There: Located just south of downtown Nashville, accessible by car with free parking available.

Closest Town for Accommodation: Hilton Nashville Green Hills offers modern amenities, including a pool and fitness center, located near shopping and dining options. Location: 3801 Cleghorn Ave, Nashville, TN 37215, Phone: (615) 297-9979.

GPS Coordinates: 36.0728° N, 86.8160° W

Interesting Facts: Radnor Lake was originally created as a reservoir for the railroad industry in the early 1900s and is now a designated State Natural Area. It is one of the best places in the area for seeing wildlife, including deer, herons, and otters.

West Tennessee

Graceland (Memphis)

Why You Should Visit: Graceland is the iconic home of Elvis Presley, offering a unique insight into the life of the "King of Rock 'n' Roll." The estate includes his mansion, private jets, and a museum filled with memorabilia, costumes, and awards. It's a must-visit for music lovers and history buffs alike, showcasing Elvis's impact on music and culture.

Website: (https://www.graceland.com)

Location: 3764 Elvis Presley Blvd, Memphis, TN 38116

What to do: Tour the mansion, museums, and exhibits on Elvis's life.

Packing list: Comfortable walking shoes, camera, and weather-appropriate clothing.

Best Time to Visit: Spring and fall for pleasant weather; avoid peak summer crowds.

Fees: Admission varies, typically ranging from $45 to $75.

How to Get There: Accessible by car with parking available; shuttle services also operate from downtown Memphis.

Closest Town for Accommodation: The Guest House at Graceland offers themed rooms, multiple dining options, and a pool. Location: 3600 Elvis Presley Blvd, Memphis, TN 38116, Phone: (901) 443-3000.

GPS Coordinates: 35.0466° N, 90.0260° W

Interesting Facts: Graceland is the second most-visited house in the United States, after the White House, and was designated a National Historic Landmark in 2006.

Beale Street (Memphis)

Why You Should Visit: Beale Street is a historic street known for its vibrant nightlife and rich musical heritage. It's a hub for blues music, with live performances, eclectic bars, and restaurants offering Southern cuisine. Beale Street is integral to the story of American music, hosting legends like B.B. King and Elvis Presley.

Website: (https://www.bealestreet.com)

Location: Beale Street, Memphis, TN 38103

What to do: Enjoy live blues music, dining, and shopping.

Packing list: Casual attire, ID for entry into bars, and comfortable shoes.

Best Time to Visit: Evenings and weekends for the best live music experience.

Fees: Generally no entry fee; costs for food, drinks, and entertainment vary.

How to Get There: Easily accessible by car or public transport; parking is available nearby.

Closest Town for Accommodation: The Peabody Memphis offers historic charm, luxury rooms, and the famous Peabody ducks. Location: 149 Union Ave, Memphis, TN 38103, Phone: (901) 529-4000.

GPS Coordinates: 35.1390° N, 90.0543° W

Interesting Facts: Beale Street was declared a National Historic Landmark in 1966 and remains a cornerstone of American blues music.

Sun Studio (Memphis)

Why You Should Visit: Sun Studio is known as the birthplace of rock 'n' roll, where legends like Elvis Presley, Johnny Cash, and Jerry Lee Lewis began their careers. The studio offers guided tours that showcase the original recording equipment and recount the stories of iconic music sessions. **Website:** (https://www.sunstudio.com)

Location: 706 Union Ave, Memphis, TN 38103

What to do: Take guided tours of the historic recording studio.

Packing list: Casual attire and a camera.

Best Time to Visit: Year-round; visit during weekdays to avoid crowds.

Fees: Tour tickets are approximately $15.

How to Get There: Located in downtown Memphis, accessible by car, foot, or public transport.

Closest Town for Accommodation: The Westin Memphis Beale Street offers modern rooms and a convenient location near major attractions. Location: 170 Lt. George W. Lee Ave, Memphis, TN 38103, Phone: (901) 334-5900.

GPS Coordinates: 35.1392° N, 90.0407° W

Interesting Facts: Sun Studio is where Elvis Presley recorded his first song, "That's All Right," in 1954, marking the birth of rock 'n' roll.

National Civil Rights Museum (Memphis)

Why You Should Visit: Located at the Lorraine Motel, where Dr. Martin Luther King Jr. was assassinated, the National Civil Rights Museum offers a powerful exploration of the American civil rights movement. The museum includes multimedia exhibits and historical artifacts that detail the struggle for racial equality in the United States.

Website: (https://www.civilrightsmuseum.org)

Location: 450 Mulberry St, Memphis, TN 38103

What to do: Explore exhibits on the civil rights movement and its key figures.

Packing list: Comfortable walking shoes and a respectful demeanor.

Best Time to Visit: Year-round; quieter during weekdays.

Fees: General admission is around $17.

How to Get There: Located in downtown Memphis, accessible by car, foot, or public transport.

Closest Town for Accommodation: Hampton Inn & Suites Memphis-Beale Street offers comfortable rooms, complimentary breakfast, and proximity to major attractions. Location: 175 Peabody Pl, Memphis, TN 38103, Phone: (901) 260-4000.

GPS Coordinates: 35.1350° N, 90.0516° W

Interesting Facts: The museum includes Room 306, where Dr. King stayed, preserved as a historic landmark.

Stax Museum of American Soul Music

Why You Should Visit: The Stax Museum celebrates the legacy of American soul music, particularly from the influential Stax Records label. The museum features over 2,000 exhibits, including instruments, stage costumes, and rare recordings. It highlights the cultural and social impact of soul music.

Website: (https://staxmuseum.com)

Location: 926 E McLemore Ave, Memphis, TN 38106

What to do: Explore exhibits on the history of Stax Records and soul music.

Packing list: Casual attire and a camera.

Best Time to Visit: Year-round; visit during weekdays for a quieter experience.

Fees: General admission is approximately $13.

How to Get There: Accessible by car or public transport, with parking available.

Closest Town for Accommodation: DoubleTree by Hilton Memphis Downtown offers comfortable accommodations, dining options, and easy access to cultural sites. Location: 185 Union Ave, Memphis, TN 38103, Phone: (901) 528-1800.

GPS Coordinates: 35.1175° N, 90.0330° W

Interesting Facts: The museum includes a replica of the Stax recording studio and Isaac Hayes's gold-trimmed Cadillac.

Memphis Zoo (Memphis)

Why You Should Visit: The Memphis Zoo is home to over 3,500 animals representing more than 500 species. The zoo offers a family-friendly experience with themed areas like Teton Trek and China, which houses giant pandas. It's an educational and entertaining destination for all ages.

Website: (https://www.memphiszoo.org)

Location: 2000 Prentiss Pl, Memphis, TN 38112

What to do: Enjoy animal exhibits, educational programs, and seasonal events.

Packing list: Comfortable walking shoes, sunscreen, and a camera.

Best Time to Visit: Spring and fall for comfortable weather and active animals.

Fees: General admission is around $18.

How to Get There: Located near downtown Memphis, accessible by car with parking available.

Closest Town for Accommodation: Sheraton Memphis Downtown Hotel offers comfortable rooms, dining options, and a fitness center. Location: 250 N Main St, Memphis, TN 38103, Phone: (901) 527-7300.

GPS Coordinates: 35.1502° N, 89.9941° W

Interesting Facts: The Memphis Zoo has been recognized as one of the top zoos in the United States and is known for its successful breeding programs for endangered species.

Shelby Farms Park (Memphis)

Why You Should Visit: Shelby Farms Park is one of the largest urban parks in the United States, covering over 4,500 acres. The park offers a wide range of outdoor activities, including hiking, biking, paddle boating, and zip-lining. It's an ideal place for nature lovers and families.

Website: (https://www.shelbyfarmspark.org)

Location: 6903 Great View Dr N, Memphis, TN 38134

What to do: Hiking, biking, paddle boating, and zip-lining.

Packing list: Outdoor gear, water, sunscreen, and a camera.

Best Time to Visit: Spring and fall for mild weather and outdoor activities.

Fees: Free entry; fees apply for certain activities and rentals.

How to Get There: reachable by car and with lots of parking.

Closest Town for Accommodation: Hyatt Place Memphis/Germantown offers comfortable accommodations with complimentary breakfast and easy access to the park. Location: 9161 Winchester Rd, Memphis, TN 38138, Phone: (901) 759-1174.

GPS Coordinates: 35.1495° N, 89.8320° W

Interesting Facts: The park includes an off-leash dog park, a large bison herd, and the Shelby Farms Greenline, a 10.65-mile urban trail connecting Midtown Memphis to the park.

Mud Island River Park (Memphis)

Why You Should Visit: Mud Island River Park offers visitors a unique experience with its Riverwalk, a scale model of the Lower Mississippi River, and the Mississippi River Museum. The park provides stunning views of the Memphis skyline and the Mississippi River, making it a popular spot for relaxation and learning about the river's history and ecology. **Website:** (https://www.mudisland.com)

Location: 125 N Front St, Memphis, TN 38103

What to do: Walk the Riverwalk, visit the museum, and enjoy river views.

Packing list: Comfortable shoes, camera, and sunscreen.

Best Time to Visit: Spring to fall for nice temperature and outdoor sports.

Fees: General admission is around $10; additional fees for certain attractions.

How to Get There: Accessible by car, foot, or monorail from downtown Memphis.

Closest Town for Accommodation: The Westin Memphis Beale Street offers modern accommodations near major attractions, with amenities including a fitness center and restaurant. Location: 170 Lt. George W. Lee Ave, Memphis, TN 38103, Phone: (901) 334-5900.

GPS Coordinates: 35.1532° N, 90.0531° W

Interesting Facts: The Riverwalk model stretches for five blocks and is one of the most comprehensive representations of the river, from Cairo, Illinois, to the Gulf of Mexico.

Pink Palace Museum (Memphis)

Why You Should Visit: The Pink Palace Museum is one of the largest science and history museums in the Southeast. It features exhibits on natural history, cultural history, and science, as well as a planetarium and IMAX theater. The museum is housed in a historic pink mansion, offering a blend of educational and entertaining experiences.

Website: (https://www.memphismuseums.org/pink-palace-museum/) **Location:** 3050 Central Ave, Memphis, TN 38111

What to do: Explore exhibits, watch planetarium shows, and see IMAX films.

Packing list: Comfortable attire, camera, and curiosity.

Best Time to Visit: Year-round; ideal for indoor activities, especially during hot or rainy days.

Fees: $15; additional fees for IMAX and planetarium shows.

How to Get There: Accessible by car with parking available; public transportation options also exist.

Closest Town for Accommodation: Hampton Inn & Suites Memphis-Shady Grove offers comfortable accommodations, complimentary breakfast, and a fitness center. Location: 962 S Shady Grove Rd, Memphis, TN 38120, Phone: (901) 762-0056.

GPS Coordinates: 35.1225° N, 89.9636° W

Interesting Facts: The mansion was originally the home of Clarence Saunders, founder of the Piggly Wiggly grocery chain, and is known for its distinctive pink Georgian marble facade.

Casey Jones Village (Jackson)

Why You Should Visit: Casey Jones Village is a historic site dedicated to the famous railroad engineer Casey Jones, who became a folk hero for his bravery in saving lives during a train accident. The village includes the Casey Jones Home & Railroad Museum, a country store, and a classic Southern restaurant, offering a charming glimpse into American railroad history and Southern culture. **Website:** (https://www.caseyjones.com)

Location: 56 Casey Jones Ln, Jackson, TN 38305

What to do: Visit the museum, shop at the country store, and dine at the restaurant.

Packing list: Comfortable attire and a camera.

Best Time to Visit: Spring to fall for pleasant weather; suitable year-round for indoor activities.

Fees: Museum admission is around $6; entry to the village is free.

How to Get There: Located in Jackson, TN, accessible by car with parking available.

Closest Town for Accommodation: DoubleTree by Hilton Hotel Jackson offers comfortable rooms, dining options, and easy access to the village. Location: 1770 US-45 BYP, Jackson, TN 38305, Phone: (731) 664-6900.

GPS Coordinates: 35.6429° N, 88.8235° W

Interesting Facts: Casey Jones Village includes the Casey Jones Railroad Museum, which houses Jones's personal belongings and offers detailed insights into his life and the history of American railroads.

East Tennessee

Tennessee Aquarium (Chattanooga)

Why You Should Visit: The Tennessee Aquarium is one of the top-rated aquariums in the United States, showcasing a diverse range of aquatic life from freshwater to ocean environments. It features interactive exhibits and special programs, providing an educational and engaging experience for visitors of all ages.

Website: [Tennessee Aquarium](https://www.tnaqua.org)

Location: 1 Broad St, Chattanooga, TN 37402

What to do: Explore exhibits featuring marine and freshwater creatures, and watch IMAX films.

Packing list: Comfortable walking shoes, camera, and light jacket for indoor climate control.

Best Time to Visit: Open year-round; weekdays are less crowded.

Fees: General admission is around $35 for adults.

How to Get There: Accessible by car, with parking available nearby; also reachable by public transit.

Closest Town for Accommodation: The Westin Chattanooga offers modern accommodations, a rooftop pool, and a fitness center. Location: 801 Pine St, Chattanooga, TN 37402, Phone: (423) 531-4653.

GPS Coordinates: 35.0553° N, 85.3102° W

Interesting Facts: The Tennessee Aquarium is home to more than 12,000 animals, including otters, penguins, and a variety of fish species.

Lookout Mountain (Chattanooga)

Why You Should Visit: Lookout Mountain offers breathtaking views and is home to several popular attractions, including Ruby Falls and Rock City. It's a natural wonder that provides outdoor adventure, scenic beauty, and historical significance.

Website: (https://www.lookoutmountain.com)

Location: Lookout Mountain, Chattanooga, TN

What to do: Hiking, sightseeing, and exploring natural attractions.

Packing list: Hiking shoes, water, camera, and weather-appropriate clothing.

Best Time to Visit: Spring and fall for mild weather and clear views.

Fees: Varies by specific attraction (e.g., Ruby Falls, Rock City).

How to Get There: Accessible by car; parking available at various attractions.

Closest Town for Accommodation: Chanticleer Inn Bed & Breakfast offers charming accommodations with personalized service and easy access to Lookout Mountain attractions. Location: 1300 Mockingbird Ln, Lookout Mountain, GA 30750, Phone: (706) 820-2002.

GPS Coordinates: 34.9745° N, 85.3549° W

Interesting Facts: Lookout Mountain played a significant role during the Civil War and is known for the "Battle Above the Clouds."

Ruby Falls (Chattanooga)

Why You Should Visit: Ruby Falls is a spectacular underground waterfall located deep inside Lookout Mountain. It is the tallest and deepest publicly accessible waterfall in the United States, offering guided tours that showcase its stunning natural beauty.

Website: (https://www.rubyfalls.com)

Location: 1720 South Scenic Hwy, Chattanooga, TN 37409

What to do: Take a guided tour to see the waterfall and cave formations.

Packing list: Comfortable shoes, a light jacket, and a camera.

Best Time to Visit: Open year-round; early mornings or weekdays are less crowded.

Fees: General admission is around $25.

How to Get There: Accessible by car; parking is available.

Closest Town for Accommodation: The Chattanoogan Hotel, Curio Collection by Hilton offers modern amenities, dining, and a spa, located in downtown Chattanooga. Location: 1201 Broad St, Chattanooga, TN 37402, Phone: (423) 756-3400.

GPS Coordinates: 35.0246° N, 85.3403° W

Interesting Facts: Ruby Falls was discovered by accident in 1928 during an attempt to find an alternative entrance to Lookout Mountain Cave.

Rock City (Chattanooga)

Why You Should Visit: Rock City is a popular tourist attraction featuring massive ancient rock formations, gardens with over 400 native plant species, and breathtaking panoramic views from the "Lover's Leap" overlook. It's famous for the "See Rock City" barns painted across the country.

Website: (https://www.seerockcity.com)

Location: 1400 Patten Rd, Lookout Mountain, GA 30750

What to do: Walk the Enchanted Trail, explore rock formations, and enjoy the scenic views.

Packing list: Comfortable walking shoes, camera, and weather-appropriate clothing.

Best Time to Visit: Spring and fall for optimal weather and garden views.

Fees: General admission is around $22.

How to Get There: Accessible by automobile, with parking provided.

Closest Town for Accommodation: Chanticleer Inn Bed & Breakfast offers charming accommodations with personalized service and proximity to Rock City. Location: 1300 Mockingbird Ln, Lookout Mountain, GA 30750, Phone: (706) 820-2002.

GPS Coordinates: 34.9729° N, 85.3619° W

Interesting Facts: Rock City's "See Seven States" viewpoint allows visitors to view seven U.S. states on a clear day.

Incline Railway (Chattanooga)

Why You Should Visit: The Incline Railway, known as "America's Most Amazing Mile," offers a unique and historic experience as it travels up Lookout Mountain at a steep incline. It provides stunning views of the surrounding landscape and is one of the world's steepest passenger railways.

Website: (https://ridetheincline.com)

Location: 3917 St Elmo Ave, Chattanooga, TN 37409

What to do: Ride the railway for scenic views and explore the area at the top.

Packing list: Camera, light jacket, and comfortable shoes.

Best Time to Visit: Spring and fall for the best visibility and weather.

Fees: Round-trip tickets are around $15.

How to Get There: Accessible by car, with parking available at the stations.

Closest Town for Accommodation: The Read House offers historic charm and modern amenities, including a pool and dining options, in downtown Chattanooga. Location: 107 W M.L.K. Blvd, Chattanooga, TN 37402, Phone: (423) 266-4121.

GPS Coordinates: 35.0028° N, 85.3426° W

Interesting Facts: The Incline Railway has been in operation since 1895 and provides a unique view of the historic battlefields and landscapes of Chattanooga.

Chattanooga Choo Choo (Chattanooga)

Why You Should Visit: The Chattanooga Choo Choo is a historic train station turned hotel and entertainment complex. It's named after the famous Glenn Miller song and features vintage railcars, gardens, restaurants, and live music, making it a nostalgic destination for visitors.

Website: (https://www.choochoo.com)

Location: 1400 Market St, Chattanooga, TN 37402

What to do: Explore the historic train station, dine at restaurants, and enjoy entertainment.

Packing list: Casual attire, camera, and comfortable shoes.

Best Time to Visit: Year-round; check for special events and performances.

Fees: Free to explore the complex; accommodation and dining are extra.

How to Get There: Located in downtown Chattanooga, accessible by car and public transport.

Closest Town for Accommodation: Chattanooga Choo Choo Hotel offers unique accommodations in renovated train cars and standard rooms, with dining and entertainment on-site. Location: 1400 Market St, Chattanooga, TN 37402, Phone: (423) 266-5000.

GPS Coordinates: 35.0368° N, 85.3090° W

Interesting Facts: The Chattanooga Choo Choo was the first train to provide non-stop service from Cincinnati to Chattanooga in the 1880s.

Hunter Museum of American Art

Why You Should Visit: The Hunter Museum of American Art features a diverse collection of American art from the Colonial period to contemporary works. Located on a bluff overlooking the Tennessee River, the museum combines historic architecture with modern design, offering a unique cultural experience.

Website: (https://www.huntermuseum.org)

Location: 10 Bluff View Ave, Chattanooga, TN 37403

What to do: Explore art exhibits and enjoy river views.

Packing list: Casual attire and a camera.

Best Time to Visit: Open year-round; ideal for indoor cultural experiences.

Fees: General admission is around $20.

How to Get There: Located near downtown Chattanooga, accessible by car or public transit.

Closest Town for Accommodation: Bluff View Inn offers charming accommodations with scenic views, dining options, and proximity to the museum. Location: 411 E 2nd St, Chattanooga, TN 37403, Phone: (423) 265-5033.

GPS Coordinates: 35.0552° N, 85.3059° W

Interesting Facts: The museum's collection includes works by famous American artists such as Winslow Homer, Mary Cassatt, and Thomas Cole.

Tennessee Valley Railroad Museum

Why You Should Visit: The Tennessee Valley Railroad Museum is a living museum dedicated to preserving railway history. It offers scenic train rides through picturesque landscapes and showcases restored vintage railcars and locomotives. This experience is ideal for history enthusiasts and families looking to enjoy a nostalgic journey.

Website: (https://www.tvrail.com)

Location: 4119 Cromwell Rd, Chattanooga, TN 37421

What to do: Take scenic train rides and explore the museum exhibits.

Packing list: Comfortable attire, camera, and weather-appropriate clothing.

Best Time to Visit: Spring and fall for the best scenic views and comfortable weather.

Fees: Train ride tickets start at around $20 for adults.

How to Get There: Accessible by automobile, with parking provided.

Closest Town for Accommodation: Hampton Inn Chattanooga-North/Ooltewah offers comfortable accommodations, complimentary breakfast, and easy access to the museum. Location: 6145 Weir Way, Ooltewah, TN 37363, Phone: (423) 305-6800.

GPS Coordinates: 35.0651° N, 85.1950° W

Interesting Facts: The museum operates the only regularly scheduled, full-sized train ride in Tennessee, providing educational and scenic experiences.

Bluff View Art District (Chattanooga)

Why You Should Visit: The Bluff View Art District is a unique area in Chattanooga that combines art, culture, and scenic views. This riverside district features art galleries, a sculpture garden, local eateries, and charming bed-and-breakfast accommodations. It's an ideal spot for a leisurely day of exploration and appreciation of the arts.

Website: (https://bluffviewartdistrict.com)

Location: 411 E 2nd St, Chattanooga, TN 37403

What to do: Visit art galleries, dine at local restaurants, and enjoy river views.

Packing list: Casual attire, comfortable shoes, and a camera.

Best Time to Visit: Year-round; spring and fall are ideal for outdoor activities.

Fees:costs vary for dining and accommodations.

How to Get There: Located in downtown Chattanooga, accessible by car or public transport.

Closest Town for Accommodation: Bluff View Inn offers charming accommodations with beautiful views, dining options, and proximity to galleries and attractions. Location: 411 E 2nd St, Chattanooga, TN 37403, Phone: (423) 265-5033.

GPS Coordinates: 35.0552° N, 85.3059° W

Interesting Facts: The Bluff View Art District includes the Hunter Museum of American Art, the River Gallery Sculpture Garden, and the Back Inn Café, known for its fine dining.

Walnut Street Bridge (Chattanooga)

Why You Should Visit: The Walnut Street Bridge is one of the longest pedestrian bridges in the world, offering stunning views of the Tennessee River and the city of Chattanooga. It is a popular spot for walking, jogging, and enjoying scenic vistas, especially during sunset. The bridge connects the downtown area with the North Shore, providing easy access to parks, shops, and restaurants.

Website:(https://www.visitchattanooga.com/listing/walnut-street-bridge/2139/)

Location: Walnut St, Chattanooga, TN 37403

What to do: Walk, jog, or cycle across the bridge and enjoy river and city views.

Packing list: Comfortable shoes, camera, and weather-appropriate clothing.

Best Time to Visit: Spring and fall for comfortable weather and scenic views.

Fees: Free to access.

How to Get There: Accessible from both downtown Chattanooga and the North Shore by foot, bike, or car.

Closest Town for Accommodation: The Edwin Hotel, Autograph Collection offers luxury accommodations, rooftop dining, and a spa, located near the bridge. Location: 102 Walnut

St, Chattanooga, TN 37403, Phone: (423) 713-5900. **GPS Coordinates:** 35.0563° N, 85.3051° W

Interesting Facts: Originally built in 1890, the Walnut Street Bridge was restored in the 1990s and has become a beloved landmark and a central part of Chattanooga's riverfront revitalization efforts.

Knoxville and Surroundings

Market Square (Knoxville)

Why You Should Visit: Market Square is the heart of downtown Knoxville, offering a vibrant mix of shops, restaurants, and cultural events. This historic square is a gathering place for locals and visitors, hosting farmers' markets, concerts, and festivals. It's an excellent spot for dining, shopping, and experiencing local culture.

Website:(https://www.visitknoxville.com/experience/areas/market-square/)

Location: Market Square, Knoxville, TN 37902

What to do: Enjoy shopping, dining, and live events.

Packing list: Comfortable walking shoes, camera, and weather-appropriate attire.

Best Time to Visit: Spring to fall for outdoor events.

Fees: Free to explore; costs vary by activity and vendor.

How to Get There: Accessible by car, with nearby parking garages; also reachable by public transport.

Closest Town for Accommodation: The Tennessean Hotel offers luxurious accommodations with modern amenities, dining options, and stunning views of downtown

Knoxville. Location: 531 Henley St, Knoxville, TN 37902, Phone: (865) 232-1800. **GPS Coordinates:** 35.9648° N, 83.9193° W

Interesting Facts: Market Square has been a hub of community life since the 1850s and has been revitalized to include modern amenities while preserving its historic charm.

Sunsphere (Knoxville)

Why You Should Visit: The Sunsphere is a unique landmark from the 1982 World's Fair, offering a 360-degree view of Knoxville and the surrounding area from its observation deck. It stands as a symbol of the city and provides a fascinating glimpse into Knoxville's history and development.

Website: (https://www.sunsphereknoxville.com)

Location: 810 Clinch Ave, Knoxville, TN 37902

What to do: Visit the observation deck for panoramic city views.

Packing list: Camera, comfortable shoes, and a light jacket for higher altitudes.

Best Time to Visit: Spring and autumn for nice temperatures and clear sky.

Fees: Admission is typically free; sometimes a small fee for special events.

How to Get There: Located in World's Fair Park, accessible by car or public transport.

Closest Town for Accommodation: Hyatt Place Knoxville/Downtown offers modern amenities, including a fitness center and complimentary breakfast, located near many attractions. Location: 530 S Gay St, Knoxville, TN 37902, Phone: (865) 544-9977.

GPS Coordinates: 35.9606° N, 83.9210° W

Interesting Facts: The Sunsphere's gold-tinted windows contain actual gold dust, and the structure was built as a symbol of energy and optimism for the 1982 World's Fair.

Knoxville Museum of Art (Knoxville)

Why You Should Visit: The Knoxville Museum of Art (KMA) showcases the art and artists of East Tennessee, along with a rotating selection of contemporary and traditional works from around the world. The museum emphasizes regional art and cultural heritage, offering a variety of exhibitions and educational programs.

Website: (https://www.knoxart.org)

Location: 1050 World's Fair Park Dr, Knoxville, TN 37916

What to do: Explore art exhibitions and participate in educational programs.

Packing list: Casual attire and a camera.

Best Time to Visit: Year-round; ideal for indoor activities, especially during rainy or hot weather.

Fees: Free admission; donations appreciated.

How to Get There: Located in World's Fair Park, accessible by car or public transport.

Closest Town for Accommodation: The Tennessean Hotel offers luxury accommodations, dining, and a central location near the museum and other downtown attractions. Location: 531 Henley St, Knoxville, TN 37902, Phone: (865) 232-1800.

GPS Coordinates: 35.9655° N, 83.9247° W

Interesting Facts: KMA's permanent collection includes the largest figural glass installation in the world, created by artist Richard Jolley.

World's Fair Park (Knoxville)

Why You Should Visit: World's Fair Park, the site of the 1982 World's Fair, is a vibrant green space in the heart of Knoxville. It features the iconic Sunsphere, interactive fountains, and outdoor concert venues. It's an ideal spot for picnicking, walking, and enjoying outdoor events.

Website: (https://www.worldsfairpark.org)

Location: 963 World's Fair Park Dr, Knoxville, TN 37916

What to do: Enjoy the fountains, walkways, and outdoor concerts.

Packing list: Comfortable shoes, picnic essentials, and sunscreen.

Best Time to Visit: Spring to fall for outdoor activities and events.

Fees: Free entry; costs vary for special events.

How to Get There: Accessible by car, with nearby parking; also reachable by public transit.

Closest Town for Accommodation: Cumberland House Knoxville, Tapestry Collection by Hilton offers comfortable rooms, dining, and a convenient location near World's Fair Park. Location: 1109 White Ave, Knoxville, TN 37916, Phone: (865) 971-4663.

GPS Coordinates: 35.9625° N, 83.9243° W

Interesting Facts: The park was developed for the 1982 World's Fair, themed "Energy Turns the World," and continues to host events celebrating innovation and culture.

Ijams Nature Center (Knoxville)

Why You Should Visit: Ijams Nature Center is a 315-acre urban green space offering a range of outdoor activities, including hiking, wildlife observation, and water sports. It's a haven for nature lovers and families, with educational programs and a focus on environmental conservation.

Website: [Ijams Nature Center](https://www.ijams.org)

Location: 2915 Island Home Ave, Knoxville, TN 37920

What to do: Hiking, wildlife viewing, and kayaking.

Packing list: Outdoor gear, water, sunscreen, and a camera.

Best Time to Visit: Spring to fall for the best weather and outdoor activities.

Fees: Free entry; fees for certain activities like canoe rentals.

How to Get There: Accessible by car, with parking available on-site.

Closest Town for Accommodation: Graduate Knoxville offers stylish accommodations with a university theme, located near the University of Tennessee campus. Location: 1706 Cumberland Ave, Knoxville, TN 37916, Phone: (865) 437-5500.

GPS Coordinates: 35.9527° N, 83.8778° W

Interesting Facts: Ijams Nature Center began as a bird sanctuary in the early 20th century and has grown to include diverse habitats like wetlands, forests, and meadows.

Tennessee Theatre (Knoxville)

Why You Should Visit: The Tennessee Theatre, known as the "Grand Entertainment Palace of the South," is a beautifully restored historic venue offering a wide range of performances, including concerts, movies, and Broadway shows. The theater's ornate interior and rich history make it a cultural treasure.

Website: (https://www.tennesseetheatre.com)

Location: 604 S Gay St, Knoxville, TN 37902

What to do: Attend live performances, including concerts and theatrical productions.

Packing list: Casual to formal attire, depending on the event.

Best Time to Visit: Year-round; check the schedule for events.

Fees: Ticket prices vary by event.

How to Get There: Located in downtown Knoxville, accessible by car or public transport.

Closest Town for Accommodation: The Oliver Hotel offers boutique accommodations with a historic charm, located in downtown Knoxville near the Tennessee Theatre. Location: 407 Union Ave, Knoxville, TN 37902, Phone: (865) 521-0050.

GPS Coordinates: 35.9641° N, 83.9199° W

Interesting Facts: The Tennessee Theatre opened in 1928 and has been restored to its original splendor, featuring a Wurlitzer organ and Spanish-Moorish architectural details.

McClung Museum of Natural History & Culture (Knoxville)

Why You Should Visit: The McClung Museum of Natural History & Culture offers fascinating exhibits on archaeology, geology, and natural history. Located on the University of Tennessee campus, the museum provides educational programs and a diverse collection of artifacts, including ancient fossils and Native American artifacts.

Website: (https://mcclungmuseum.utk.edu)

Location: 1327 Circle Park Dr, Knoxville, TN 37996

What to do: Explore exhibits on natural history and cultural artifacts.

Packing list: Casual attire and a camera.

Best Time to Visit: Year-round; ideal for indoor activities.

Fees: Free admission; donations appreciated.

How to Get There: Located on the University of Tennessee campus, accessible by car and public transport.

Closest Town for Accommodation: Hilton Knoxville offers modern accommodations, dining, and a rooftop pool, located near the University of Tennessee campus. Location: 501 W Church Ave, Knoxville, TN 37902, Phone: (865) 523-2300.

GPS Coordinates: 35.9511° N, 83.9290° W

Interesting Facts: The McClung Museum's collections include items from around the world, with a special focus on the Southeastern United States.

Knoxville Botanical Garden and Arboretum (Knoxville)

Why You Should Visit: The Knoxville Botanical Garden and Arboretum is a stunning 47-acre garden offering a diverse array of plant collections, walking trails, and historic horticultural features. It's a peaceful retreat perfect for nature lovers, providing educational opportunities and a beautiful setting for leisurely walks.

Website: (https://knoxgarden.org)

Location: 2743 Wimpole Ave, Knoxville, TN 37914

What to do: Explore themed gardens, walk the trails, and enjoy the scenic views.

Packing list: Comfortable shoes, water, and a camera.

Best Time to Visit: Spring and summer for vibrant blooms and garden events.

Fees: Free admission; donations appreciated.

How to Get There: Accessible by car with on-site parking available.

Closest Town for Accommodation: Crowne Plaza Knoxville Downtown University offers comfortable accommodations, dining, and a fitness center, located near the gardens and other attractions. Location: 401 W Summit Hill Dr, Knoxville, TN 37902, Phone: (865) 522-2600.

GPS Coordinates: 35.9823° N, 83.8915° W

Interesting Facts: The garden features the historic Howell Nurseries, which have been part of the community for over 200 years.

Neyland Stadium (Knoxville)

Why You Should Visit: Neyland Stadium is one of the most iconic college football stadiums in the United States, home to the University of Tennessee Volunteers. With a seating capacity of over 100,000, it provides an electrifying atmosphere for football games and events, showcasing the passion and tradition of college sports.

Location: 1235 Phillip Fulmer Way SW, Knoxville, TN 37996

What to do: Attend University of Tennessee football games and special events.

Packing list: Team colors, comfortable attire, and a camera.

Best Time to Visit: Fall, during the college football season.

Fees: Ticket prices vary by game and seat location.

How to Get There: Located on the University of Tennessee campus, accessible by car and public transport; parking can be challenging on game days.

Closest Town for Accommodation: Graduate Knoxville offers stylish, university-themed accommodations, located near the stadium and campus. Location: 1706 Cumberland Ave, Knoxville, TN 37916, Phone: (865) 437-5500.

GPS Coordinates: 35.9550° N, 83.9250° W

Interesting Facts: Named after former head coach Robert Neyland, the stadium has undergone numerous expansions since its opening in 1921, making it one of the largest stadiums in the country.

Knoxville Zoo (Knoxville)

Why You Should Visit: Knoxville Zoo, officially known as Zoo Knoxville, is a beloved destination featuring a wide variety of animals and engaging exhibits. It's known for its conservation efforts, particularly with red pandas and African elephants, and offers educational programs and interactive experiences for visitors.

Website: [Zoo Knoxville](https://www.zooknoxville.org)

Location: 3500 Knoxville Zoo Dr, Knoxville, TN 37914

What to do: Explore animal exhibits, participate in interactive experiences, and attend educational programs.

Packing list: Comfortable walking shoes, sunscreen, water, and a camera.

Best Time to Visit: Spring and autumn are optimal seasons for animals that are active and enjoy moderate weather.

Fees: General admission is around $20 for adults.

How to Get There: Accessible by car.

Closest Town for Accommodation: Hampton Inn & Suites Knoxville-Downtown offers comfortable accommodations, complimentary breakfast, and easy access to the zoo and other attractions. Location: 618 W Main St, Knoxville, TN 37902, Phone: (865) 522-5400.

GPS Coordinates: 35.9711° N, 83.8816° W

Interesting Facts: Zoo Knoxville is known for its successful breeding programs, particularly for endangered species like the red panda, and hosts annual events like the "Boo at the Zoo" Halloween celebration.

Great Smoky Mountains National Park

Cades Cove

Why You Should Visit: Cades Cove is a lush valley surrounded by mountains, offering some of the best opportunities for wildlife viewing in the Great Smoky Mountains National Park. It features historical structures like log cabins, churches, and a grist mill, providing a glimpse into the region's past. The 11-mile loop road around the cove is popular for driving, biking, and hiking.

Website:(https://www.nps.gov/grsm/planyourvisit/cadescove.htm)

Location: Cades Cove, TN 37882

What to do: Wildlife viewing, hiking, and exploring historical sites.

Packing list: Binoculars, camera, water, and comfortable walking shoes.

Best Time to Visit: Spring and fall for beautiful foliage and wildlife activity.

Fees: Free entrance; rental fees for bikes and other activities may apply.

How to Get There: Accessible by car via Laurel Creek Road from Townsend, TN.

Closest Town for Accommodation: Townsend Gateway Inn offers cozy accommodations with modern amenities, located near the park entrance. Location: 8270 State Hwy 73, Townsend, TN 37882, Phone: (865) 238-0123.

GPS Coordinates: 35.6024° N, 83.7766° W

Interesting Facts: Cades Cove was once a thriving community, with settlers arriving in the early 1800s. It now serves as a window into the cultural history of the region.

Clingmans Dome

Why You Should Visit: Clingmans Dome is the highest point in the Great Smoky Mountains National Park and the third highest peak east of the Mississippi River. The observation tower at the summit offers stunning 360-degree views of the Smokies. It's a must-visit for breathtaking scenery and an accessible way to experience high elevations.

Website:(https://www.nps.gov/grsm/planyourvisit/clingma nsdome.htm)

Location: Clingmans Dome Rd, Bryson City, NC 28713

What to do: Hiking to the observation tower and enjoying panoramic views.

Packing list: Warm clothing (temperatures can be much cooler), camera, and water.

Best Time to Visit: Late spring to early fall for clear views.

Fees: Free entrance; parking fees may apply.

How to Get There: Accessible by car via Clingmans Dome Road, with a short hike to the summit.

Closest Town for Accommodation: Cherokee Grand Hotel offers comfortable rooms and amenities, located in Cherokee, NC, near the park entrance. Location: 196 Paint Town Rd, Cherokee, NC 28719, Phone: (828) 497-0050.

GPS Coordinates: 35.5628° N, 83.4986° W

Interesting Facts: Clingmans Dome is named after Thomas Lanier Clingman, a U.S. senator and explorer who measured many Southern Appalachian peaks.

Roaring Fork Motor Nature Trail

Why You Should Visit: The Roaring Fork Motor Nature Trail is a scenic loop road that offers a peaceful drive through a lush forest, waterfalls, and historic buildings. It's one of the best places to experience the natural beauty of the Smokies up close, with opportunities for short hikes and nature photography.

Website:(https://www.nps.gov/grsm/planyourvisit/roaringf ork.htm)

Location: Roaring Fork Motor Nature Trail, Gatlinburg, TN 37738

What to do: Scenic driving, hiking, and exploring historic sites.

Packing list: Camera, binoculars, water, and comfortable shoes.

Best Time to Visit: Spring and fall for beautiful foliage and fewer crowds.

Fees: Free entrance; parking fees may apply.

How to Get There: Accessible by car from downtown Gatlinburg; road is one-way and narrow.

Closest Town for Accommodation: The Park Vista - a DoubleTree by Hilton Hotel offers stunning mountain views, modern amenities, and easy access to Gatlinburg attractions. Location: 705 Cherokee Orchard Rd, Gatlinburg, TN 37738, Phone: (865) 436-9211.

GPS Coordinates: 35.6764° N, 83.4698° W

Interesting Facts: Roaring Fork is named after a mountain stream that "roars" during heavy rains, highlighting the area's rich natural beauty.

Laurel Falls Trail

Why You Should Visit: Laurel Falls Trail is one of the most popular hiking trails in the Great Smoky Mountains National Park, leading to a beautiful 80-foot waterfall. The trail is relatively easy and paved, making it accessible for most visitors, including families with young children.

Website:(https://www.nps.gov/grsm/planyourvisit/laurel-falls.htm)

Location: Laurel Falls Trailhead, Little River Rd, Gatlinburg, TN 37738

What to do: Hiking and nature photography.

Packing list: Sturdy shoes, water, and a camera.

Best Time to Visit: Spring and fall for pleasant weather and water flow.

Fees: Free entrance; parking fees may apply.

How to Get There: Accessible by car via Little River Road; parking can be limited.

Closest Town for Accommodation: Margaritaville Resort Gatlinburg offers a tropical-themed stay with amenities including a spa and dining, located near the park entrance. Location: 539 Parkway, Gatlinburg, TN 37738, Phone: (888) 447-0222.

GPS Coordinates: 35.6729° N, 83.5825° W

Interesting Facts: The trail was named after the mountain laurel shrubs that bloom along the route, offering a stunning display in spring.

Newfound Gap

Why You Should Visit: Newfound Gap offers breathtaking views of the Smokies and serves as a popular starting point for exploring the park. The site includes a scenic overlook, a monument to President Franklin D. Roosevelt, and the Appalachian Trail, making it a hub for sightseeing and hiking.

Website:(https://www.nps.gov/grsm/planyourvisit/newfoun d-gap.htm)

Location: Newfound Gap Rd, Gatlinburg, TN 37738

What to do: Sightseeing, hiking, and photography.

Packing list: Warm clothing, camera, and water.

Best Time to Visit: Year-round; road conditions can vary in winter.

Fees: Free entrance; parking fees may apply.

How to Get There: Accessible by car via Newfound Gap Road (U.S. Highway 441).

Closest Town for Accommodation: Gatlinburg Inn offers cozy accommodations with a historic charm, located near the park's entrance. Location: 755 Parkway, Gatlinburg, TN 37738, Phone: (865) 436-5133.

GPS Coordinates: 35.6117° N, 83.4250° W

Interesting Facts: At an elevation of 5,046 feet, Newfound Gap provides a unique perspective on the diverse ecosystems of the Smokies.

Alum Cave Trail

Why You Should Visit: Alum Cave Trail is one of the most popular trails in the park, offering unique geological features and stunning views. The trail leads to Alum Cave Bluffs and continues to Mount LeConte, one of the highest peaks in the Smokies. It's a moderately strenuous hike, perfect for those looking for a rewarding adventure.

Website: (https://www.nps.gov/grsm/planyourvisit/alum-cave.htm)

Location: Alum Cave Trailhead, Newfound Gap Rd, Gatlinburg, TN 37738

What to do: Hiking and nature photography.

Packing list: Hiking boots, water, snacks, and a camera.

Best Time to Visit: Spring to fall for the best weather and trail conditions.

Fees: Free entrance; parking fees may apply.

How to Get There: Accessible by car via Newfound Gap Road; trailhead parking available.

Closest Town for Accommodation: Greystone Lodge on the River offers comfortable accommodations with amenities like a fitness center and breakfast, located near downtown Gatlinburg. Location: 559 Parkway, Gatlinburg, TN 37738, Phone: (865) 436-5621.

GPS Coordinates: 35.6293° N, 83.4308° W

Interesting Facts: Despite its name, Alum Cave is actually a concave bluff, known for its Epsom salt deposits and stunning views of the surrounding mountains.

Elkmont Ghost Town

Why You Should Visit: Elkmont Ghost Town offers a fascinating glimpse into the park's history as a former logging community turned resort town. Visitors can explore abandoned cabins and learn about the area's rich history, including its transformation from a bustling settlement to a deserted village. It's a unique destination for history buffs and those interested in the cultural heritage of the Smokies.

Website:(https://www.nps.gov/grsm/learn/historyculture/el kmont.htm) **Location:** Elkmont, Great Smoky Mountains National Park, TN

What to do: Explore historic cabins and structures.

Packing list: Comfortable shoes, camera, and water.

Best Time to Visit: Spring to fall for comfortable weather.

Fees: Free entrance; parking fees may apply.

How to Get There: Accessible by car from Little River Road; follow signs to the Elkmont Campground area.

Closest Town for Accommodation: Gatlinburg Town Square by Exploria Resorts offers comfortable accommodations with amenities like an indoor pool and fitness center, located near downtown Gatlinburg. Location: 414 Historic Nature Trail, Gatlinburg, TN 37738, Phone: (865) 436-2039.

GPS Coordinates: 35.6595° N, 83.5821° W

Interesting Facts: Elkmont was once a popular vacation destination for wealthy Knoxville residents, and the remnants of the Wonderland Hotel and various cabins are still visible today.

Gatlinburg Scenic Overlook (Gatlinburg)

Why You Should Visit: The Gatlinburg Scenic Overlook offers panoramic views of the city of Gatlinburg and the surrounding Great Smoky Mountains. It's a perfect spot for photography, particularly at sunrise and sunset, and provides a serene escape to enjoy the natural beauty of the area.

Website: (https://www.gatlinburg.com/listing/gatlinburg-scenic-overlook/370/)

Location: Gatlinburg Bypass, Gatlinburg, TN 37738

What to do: Sightseeing and photography.

Packing list: Camera, binoculars, and a light jacket.

Best Time to Visit: Either in the early morning or late evening

Fees: Free access.

How to Get There: Accessible by car via the Gatlinburg Bypass; parking available at designated overlooks.

Closest Town for Accommodation: The Park Vista - a DoubleTree by Hilton Hotel offers stunning mountain views, an indoor pool, and easy access to Gatlinburg attractions. Location: 705 Cherokee Orchard Rd, Gatlinburg, TN 37738, Phone: (865) 436-9211.

GPS Coordinates: 35.7036° N, 83.5102° W

Interesting Facts: The overlook provides a great vantage point to see Gatlinburg nestled among the Smokies, especially beautiful during the fall foliage season.

Chimney Tops Trail

Why You Should Visit: Chimney Tops Trail is one of the park's most popular hikes, known for its challenging terrain and rewarding views. The trail climbs steeply to a rocky pinnacle, offering panoramic views of the surrounding mountains. It's a favorite for hikers seeking a short but strenuous hike with a big payoff.

Website:(https://www.nps.gov/grsm/planyourvisit/chimney -tops.htm)

Location: Chimney Tops Trailhead, Newfound Gap Rd, Gatlinburg, TN 37738

What to do: Hiking and photography.

Packing list: Sturdy hiking boots, water, and snacks.

Best Time to Visit: Spring to fall.

Fees: Free entrance; parking fees may apply.

How to Get There: Accessible by car.

Closest Town for Accommodation: The Lodge at Buckberry Creek offers rustic elegance with modern amenities, including a restaurant and easy access to outdoor activities. Location: 961 Campbell Lead Rd, Gatlinburg, TN 37738, Phone: (865) 430-8030.

GPS Coordinates: 35.6356° N, 83.4690° W

Interesting Facts: The trail was partially closed and rerouted after a wildfire in 2016, but it remains a popular destination for experienced hikers.

Sugarlands Visitor Center (Gatlinburg)

Why You Should Visit: The Sugarlands Visitor Center is an excellent starting point for exploring the Great Smoky Mountains National Park. It features informative exhibits on the park's natural and cultural history, a bookstore, and knowledgeable staff to assist with trip planning. Several easy trails and scenic spots are accessible from the center.

Website:(https://www.nps.gov/grsm/planyourvisit/visitorce nters.htm)

Location: 1420 Fighting Creek Gap Rd, Gatlinburg, TN 37738

What to do: Visit exhibits, watch educational films.

Packing list: Comfortable attire, camera.

Best Time to Visit: Year-round

Fees: Free entrance; donations appreciated.

How to Get There: Located near Gatlinburg, accessible by car via U.S. Highway 441.

Closest Town for Accommodation: Black Bear Inn & Suites offers comfortable rooms, a complimentary breakfast, and easy access to downtown Gatlinburg and the national park. Location: 1100 Parkway, Gatlinburg, TN 37738, Phone: (865) 436-5656.

GPS Coordinates: 35.6815° N, 83.5367° W

Interesting Facts: The center's exhibits cover the diverse plant and animal life of the park, as well as its history, making it a great educational stop for visitors of all ages.

Pigeon Forge and Gatlinburg

Dollywood (Pigeon Forge)

Why You Should Visit: Dollywood, owned by country music star Dolly Parton, is one of Tennessee's premier theme parks, offering thrilling rides, live entertainment, and traditional crafts. It's a family-friendly destination that celebrates the culture and natural beauty of the Smoky Mountains, making it a must-visit for amusement park enthusiasts and Dolly Parton fans alike. **Website:** (https://www.dollywood.com)

Location: 2700 Dollywood Parks Blvd, Pigeon Forge, TN 37863

What to do: Enjoy roller coasters, live shows, and artisan crafts.

Packing list: Comfortable clothing, sunscreen, and a camera.

Best Time to Visit: Spring and fall

Fees: $70 to $85, depending on the season.

How to Get There: Accessible by car.

Closest Town for Accommodation: DreamMore Resort and Spa offers luxurious accommodations, dining, and shuttle services to Dollywood. Location: 2525 DreamMore Way, Pigeon Forge, TN 37863, Phone: (865) 365-1900.

GPS Coordinates: 35.8053° N, 83.5308° W

Interesting Facts: Dollywood features a variety of seasonal festivals, including the Smoky Mountain Christmas and Harvest Festival, showcasing local culture and traditions.

The Island in Pigeon Forge

Why You Should Visit: The Island in Pigeon Forge is a shopping, dining, and entertainment complex featuring the Great Smoky Mountain Wheel, a large observation wheel offering stunning views. It's a lively destination perfect for families and groups, with attractions like escape rooms, a musical fountain, and unique shops.

Website: (https://islandinpigeonforge.com)

Location: 131 Island Dr, Pigeon Forge, TN 37863

What to do: Shop, dine, ride the Great Smoky Mountain Wheel, and enjoy entertainment.

Packing list: Comfortable attire, and a camera.

Best Time to Visit: Year-round.

Fees: Free entry; costs vary by attraction and activity.

How to Get There: Accessible by car.

Closest Town for Accommodation: Margaritaville Island Hotel offers themed rooms, rooftop dining, and easy access to The Island's attractions. Location: 131 The Island Dr, Pigeon Forge, TN 37863, Phone: (865) 774-2300.

GPS Coordinates: 35.8068° N, 83.5754° W

Interesting Facts: The Island features a 200-foot-tall observation wheel and a state-of-the-art fountain that performs hourly choreographed water and light shows.

Titanic Museum Attraction

Why You Should Visit: The Titanic Museum Attraction offers an immersive experience into the history of the RMS Titanic, featuring a half-scale replica of the ship and over 400 artifacts. Visitors can learn about the ship's construction, its ill-fated voyage, and the stories of its passengers, making it both educational and poignant.

Website: (https://titanicpigeonforge.com)

Location: 2134 Parkway, Pigeon Forge, TN 37863

What to do: Explore exhibits and artifacts, and learn about the Titanic's history.

Packing list: Casual attire and a camera.

Best Time to Visit: Open year-round; visit during weekdays to avoid crowds.

Fees: General admission is around $35 for adults.

How to Get There: Located on the Parkway in Pigeon Forge, accessible by car with on-site parking.

Closest Town for Accommodation: The Inn at Christmas Place offers themed accommodations, including holiday decor year-round, and amenities like a heated pool and complimentary breakfast. Location: 119 Christmas Tree Ln, Pigeon Forge, TN 37863, Phone: (865) 868-0525.

GPS Coordinates: 35.8153° N, 83.5790° W

Interesting Facts: The museum's exterior replicates the Titanic's bow, and visitors are given boarding passes with the names of actual passengers, adding a personal touch to the experience.

Smoky Mountain Alpine Coaster

Why You Should Visit: The Smoky Mountain Alpine Coaster is the longest downhill ride in the United States, offering an exhilarating experience through the Smoky Mountains. Riders control the speed of their descent, making it suitable for thrill-seekers and families alike.

Website: (https://www.smokymountainalpinecoaster.com)

Location: 867 Wears Valley Rd, Pigeon Forge, TN 37863

What to do: Ride the alpine coaster for a thrilling descent through the mountains.

Packing list: Comfortable clothing and a camera.

Best Time to Visit: Year-round; nighttime rides offer a unique experience with track lighting.

Fees: Ride tickets are around $15 for adults.

How to Get There: Accessible by car, with on-site parking available.

Closest Town for Accommodation: RiverStone Resort & Spa offers upscale accommodations, a spa, and convenient access to Pigeon Forge attractions. Location: 212 Dollywood Ln, Pigeon Forge, TN 37863, Phone: (865) 908-0660.

GPS Coordinates: 35.7853° N, 83.5971° W

Interesting Facts: The coaster operates in all weather conditions, providing a unique way to experience the Smokies in different seasons.

WonderWorks (Pigeon Forge)

Why You Should Visit: WonderWorks is an interactive science museum with over 100 hands-on exhibits designed to spark curiosity and imagination. The upside-down building is a landmark attraction in Pigeon Forge, offering activities that range from physical challenges to educational experiences.

Website: (https://www.wonderworksonline.com/pigeon-forge/)

Location: 100 Music Rd, Pigeon Forge, TN 37863

What to do: Explore interactive exhibits, including a space zone, earthquake simulator, and laser tag.

Packing list: Comfortable attire and a camera.

Best Time to Visit: Year-round; weekdays are less crowded.

Fees: General admission is around $30 for adults.

How to Get There: Located on Music Road, accessible by car with parking available.

Closest Town for Accommodation: The Inn on the River offers comfortable rooms, a complimentary breakfast, and riverside views, located near major attractions. Location: 2492 Parkway, Pigeon Forge, TN 37863, Phone: (865) 428-5500.

GPS Coordinates: 35.8120° N, 83.5754° W

Interesting Facts: The building's upside-down design simulates a fictional story where an experiment gone wrong lifted it and landed it in Pigeon Forge.

Hollywood Wax Museum (Pigeon Forge)

Why You Should Visit: The Hollywood Wax Museum features lifelike wax figures of famous celebrities and iconic film characters, allowing visitors to take photos with their favorite stars. It's an engaging and entertaining experience that appeals to fans of movies and pop culture.

Website:(https://www.hollywoodwaxentertainment.com/pigeon-forge/)

Location: 106 Showplace Blvd, Pigeon Forge, TN 37863

What to do: Pose with wax figures of celebrities and movie icons.

Packing list: Camera and casual attire.

Best Time to Visit: Open year-round; evenings can be less crowded.

Fees: General admission is around $30 for adults.

How to Get There: Located on Showplace Boulevard, accessible by car with on-site parking.

Closest Town for Accommodation: The Ramsey Hotel and Convention Center offers comfortable accommodations, an indoor pool, and easy access to Pigeon Forge attractions. Location: 3230 Parkway, Pigeon Forge, TN 37863, Phone: (865) 428-2700.

GPS Coordinates: 35.8161° N, 83.5794° W

Interesting Facts: The museum also features a Hollywood Stars Cars Museum with vehicles from famous movies and TV shows.

Alcatraz East Crime Museum

Why You Should Visit: Alcatraz East Crime Museum offers a comprehensive look at American crime history, with exhibits on famous criminals, law enforcement, forensic science, and the justice system. It's an educational and intriguing destination for those interested in true crime and criminology.

Website: (https://www.alcatrazeast.com)

Location: 2757 Parkway, Pigeon Forge, TN 37863

What to do: Explore exhibits on crime history, forensic science, and criminal psychology.

Packing list: Casual attire and a camera.

Best Time to Visit: Open year-round; visit on weekdays to avoid crowds.

Fees: General admission is around $25 for adults.

How to Get There: Located on the Parkway, accessible by car with on-site parking.

Closest Town for Accommodation: Black Fox Lodge Pigeon Forge, Tapestry Collection by Hilton offers stylish accommodations, an outdoor pool, and a convenient location near attractions. Location: 3171 Parkway, Pigeon Forge, TN 37863, Phone: (865) 774-4000.

GPS Coordinates: 35.8169° N, 83.5753° W

Interesting Facts (Continued): The museum features artifacts such as O.J. Simpson's Ford Bronco, a collection of serial killer artwork, and a gallery dedicated to the history of Alcatraz prison.

Dolly Parton's Stampede (Pigeon Forge)

Why You Should Visit: Dolly Parton's Stampede is a dinner theater experience featuring a live performance with horseback riding stunts, musical productions, and comedy. The show celebrates the American spirit and Southern charm, offering a hearty meal along with the entertainment.

Website: (https://dpstampede.com/pigeon-forge)

Location: 3849 Parkway, Pigeon Forge, TN 37863

What to do: Enjoy a live show with dinner, featuring music, stunts, and comedy.

Packing list: Casual attire suitable for dining and a show.

Best Time to Visit: Year-round; evenings for dinner shows.

Fees: Tickets range from $55 to $70, including the meal.

How to Get There: Located on the Parkway, accessible by car with ample parking.

Closest Town for Accommodation: Dollywood's DreamMore Resort and Spa offers luxurious accommodations, spa services, and shuttle access to Dollywood. Location: 2525 DreamMore Way, Pigeon Forge, TN 37863, Phone: (865) 365-1900.

GPS Coordinates: 35.7948° N, 83.5474° W

Interesting Facts: The show features a "friendly competition" between sides of the audience, creating an interactive and engaging atmosphere for all ages.

The Old Mill (Pigeon Forge)

Why You Should Visit: The Old Mill, built in 1830, is a historic gristmill still in operation today. It's a key landmark in Pigeon Forge, offering a glimpse into the area's early industrial history. The complex includes a restaurant, shops, and a general store, making it a charming spot for dining and shopping.

Website: (https://www.old-mill.com)

Location: 175 Old Mill Ave, Pigeon Forge, TN 37863

What to do: Tour the mill, dine at the Old Mill Restaurant, and shop for local goods.

Packing list: Casual attire and a camera.

Best Time to Visit: Open year-round; mornings are ideal for a quieter experience.

Fees: Free to explore; costs apply for dining and shopping.

How to Get There: Located near the Parkway, accessible by car with parking available.

Closest Town for Accommodation: The Inn on the River offers comfortable rooms, a complimentary breakfast, and scenic views of the Little Pigeon River. Location: 2492 Parkway, Pigeon Forge, TN 37863, Phone: (865) 428-5500.

GPS Coordinates: 35.7912° N, 83.5507° W

Interesting Facts: The Old Mill is listed on the National Register of Historic Places and has been a centerpiece of Pigeon Forge for nearly two centuries.

Ripley's Aquarium of the Smokies

Why You Should Visit: Ripley's Aquarium of the Smokies is a top-rated aquarium featuring a wide range of marine life exhibits, including a shark tunnel, a penguin playhouse, and interactive touch tanks. It offers educational and engaging experiences for visitors of all ages, making it a popular family destination.

Website: (https://www.ripleyaquariums.com/gatlinburg/)

Location: 88 River Rd, Gatlinburg, TN 37738

What to do: Explore marine exhibits, enjoy interactive displays, and watch live animal shows.

Packing list: Comfortable attire and a camera.

Best Time to Visit: Open year-round; visit during weekdays to avoid crowds.

Fees: General admission is around $40 for adults.

How to Get There: Located in downtown Gatlinburg, accessible by car or foot with nearby parking available.

Closest Town for Accommodation: Bearskin Lodge on the River offers cozy accommodations with rustic charm, a pool, and proximity to downtown Gatlinburg. Location: 840 River Rd, Gatlinburg, TN 37738, Phone: (865) 430-4330.

GPS Coordinates: 35.7091° N, 83.5197° W

Interesting Facts: The aquarium is home to over 10,000 sea creatures and has been recognized as one of the top aquariums in the United States by TripAdvisor.

Gatlinburg and Surroundings

Gatlinburg SkyLift Park (Gatlinburg)

Why You Should Visit: Gatlinburg SkyLift Park offers breathtaking views of the Great Smoky Mountains from its iconic chairlift and SkyBridge, the longest pedestrian suspension bridge in North America. It's an unforgettable experience for those looking to enjoy stunning landscapes and a bit of adventure.

Website: (https://www.gatlinburgskylift.com)

Location: 765 Parkway, Gatlinburg, TN 37738

What to do: Ride the SkyLift, walk the SkyBridge, and explore the SkyDeck.

Packing list: Comfortable shoes, a camera, and weather-appropriate clothing.

Best Time to Visit: Spring and fall for clear views and mild weather.

Fees: Admission ranges from $20 to $30.

How to Get There: Located in downtown Gatlinburg, accessible by car with nearby parking.

Closest Town for Accommodation: The Greystone Lodge on the River offers cozy accommodations, complimentary breakfast, and easy access to Gatlinburg attractions. Location: 559 Parkway, Gatlinburg, TN 37738, Phone: (865) 436-5621.

GPS Coordinates: 35.7111° N, 83.5180° W

Interesting Facts: The SkyBridge stretches 680 feet across a deep valley and has a glass-floor section in the middle, offering a thrilling view of the forest below.

Ober Gatlinburg (Gatlinburg)

Why You Should Visit: Ober Gatlinburg is a year-round amusement park and ski resort offering a variety of activities, including skiing, snowboarding, an alpine slide, and a wildlife encounter. It's a unique destination where visitors can enjoy both winter sports and summer fun.

Website: (https://www.obergatlinburg.com)

Location: 1339 Ski Mountain Rd, Gatlinburg, TN 37738

What to do: Skiing, snowboarding, tubing, and wildlife encounters.

Packing list: Seasonal attire, such as warm clothes for winter sports or casual clothing for summer activities.

Best Time to Visit: Winter for skiing and summer for outdoor activities.

Fees: Fees vary by activity; lift tickets and rental equipment have additional costs.

How to Get There: Accessible by car or Aerial Tramway from downtown Gatlinburg.

Closest Town for Accommodation: Glenstone Lodge offers comfortable accommodations with an indoor pool, located near Gatlinburg's attractions. Location: 504 Historic Nature Trail, Gatlinburg, TN 37738, Phone: (865) 436-9361.

GPS Coordinates: 35.7036° N, 83.5210° W

Interesting Facts: Ober Gatlinburg is Tennessee's only ski resort, featuring an ice skating rink and an alpine coaster.

Great Smoky Arts & Crafts Community

Why You Should Visit: The Great Smoky Arts & Crafts Community is the largest group of independent artisans in North America, offering handmade crafts ranging from pottery to jewelry. This 8-mile loop provides a unique shopping experience where visitors can meet the artisans and see them at work.

Website: (https://www.gatlinburgcrafts.com)

Location: 668 Glades Rd, Gatlinburg, TN 37738

What to do: Shop for handmade crafts, watch artisans at work, and enjoy local cuisine.

Packing list: Comfortable walking shoes and a shopping bag.

Best Time to Visit: Open year-round; ideal during seasonal festivals.

Fees: Free to explore; costs apply for purchases.

How to Get There: Accessible by car with free parking at most shops.

Closest Town for Accommodation: Zoder's Inn & Suites offers comfortable rooms and a complimentary breakfast, located close to the crafts community and Gatlinburg attractions. Location: 402 Parkway, Gatlinburg, TN 37738, Phone: (865) 436-5681.

GPS Coordinates: 35.7266° N, 83.4625° W

Interesting Facts: The community was established in 1937 to preserve and promote traditional Appalachian crafts.

Gatlinburg Space Needle (Gatlinburg)

Why You Should Visit: The Gatlinburg Space Needle is a 407-foot observation tower offering 360-degree views of the Smoky Mountains and Gatlinburg. It's equipped with glass elevators, providing a thrilling ascent to the observation deck where visitors can enjoy panoramic views and educational exhibits.

Website: (https://www.gatlinburgspaceneedle.com)

Location: 115 Historic Nature Trail, Gatlinburg, TN 37738

What to do: Take in the views from the observation deck and explore the arcade and theater.

Packing list: Camera and weather-appropriate attire.

Best Time to Visit: Year-round; evenings for night views.

Fees: Admission is around $15 for adults.

How to Get There: Located in downtown Gatlinburg, accessible by car with nearby parking.

Closest Town for Accommodation: Holiday Inn Club Vacations Smoky Mountain Resort offers spacious accommodations, a fitness center, and proximity to downtown attractions. Location: 404 Historic Nature Trail, Gatlinburg, TN 37738, Phone: (865) 428-8600.

GPS Coordinates: 35.7127° N, 83.5193° W

Interesting Facts: The Space Needle has a 14-story observation deck that offers some of the best views of the Smoky Mountains, especially during the fall foliage season.

Anakeesta (Gatlinburg)

Why You Should Visit: Anakeesta is an outdoor adventure park offering a range of activities, including a treetop skywalk, ziplining, and a mountain coaster. The park also features botanical gardens, dining, and shopping, making it a versatile destination for families and adventure seekers.

Website: [Anakeesta](https://www.anakeesta.com)

Location: 576 Parkway, Gatlinburg, TN 37738

What to do: Ziplining, treetop skywalk, mountain coaster, and dining.

Packing list: Comfortable attire, camera, and outdoor gear.

Best Time to Visit: Spring and fall for pleasant weather and scenic views.

Fees: General admission is around $30, with additional costs for certain activities.

How to Get There: Accessible by car, with a scenic Chondola or Ridge Rambler from downtown Gatlinburg.

Closest Town for Accommodation: Margaritaville Resort Gatlinburg offers luxurious accommodations, a spa, and dining, located near Anakeesta. Location: 539 Parkway, Gatlinburg, TN 37738, Phone: (888) 447-0222.

GPS Coordinates: 35.7113° N, 83.5182° W

Interesting Facts: Anakeesta's name comes from the Cherokee word for "place of the balsams," reflecting the area's rich Native American heritage.

Ripley's Believe It or Not! (Gatlinburg)

Why You Should Visit: Ripley's Believe It or Not! in Gatlinburg showcases oddities and unusual artifacts from around the world. This family-friendly attraction is filled with strange exhibits, interactive displays, and unique curiosities that challenge the imagination and entertain visitors of all ages.

Website: (https://www.ripleys.com/gatlinburg/)

Location: 800 Parkway, Gatlinburg, TN 37738

What to do: Explore interactive exhibits and see bizarre artifacts.

Packing list: Casual attire and a camera.

Best Time to Visit: Open year-round; weekdays are less crowded.

Fees: General admission is around $20 for adults.

How to Get There: Located in downtown Gatlinburg, accessible by car with nearby parking.

Closest Town for Accommodation: River Terrace Resort and Convention Center offers comfortable accommodations and amenities like an outdoor pool, located near Ripley's attractions. Location: 240 River Rd, Gatlinburg, TN 37738, Phone: (865) 436-5161.

GPS Coordinates: 35.7124° N, 83.5157° W

Interesting Facts: The Gatlinburg location is one of the oldest Ripley's Believe It or Not! museums, featuring over 500 exhibits and artifacts.

Gatlinburg Mountain Coaster

Why You Should Visit: The Gatlinburg Mountain Coaster offers a thrilling ride through the Smoky Mountains, where riders control their own speed. The coaster operates year-round, providing a unique way to experience the natural beauty of the area from a different perspective.

Website: (https://gatlinburgmountaincoaster.com)

Location: 306 Parkway, Gatlinburg, TN 37738

What to do: Ride the alpine coaster for a thrilling experience.**Packing list:** Comfortable attire and a camera.

Best Time to Visit: Year-round; nighttime rides offer a unique experience with illuminated tracks.

Fees: Ride tickets are around $15 for adults.

How to Get There: Accessible by car, with on-site parking available.

Closest Town for Accommodation: Bearskin Lodge on the River offers rustic accommodations with modern amenities, located near the mountain coaster. Location: 840 River Rd, Gatlinburg, TN 37738, Phone: (865) 430-4330.

GPS Coordinates: 35.7072° N, 83.5204° W

Interesting Facts: The Gatlinburg Mountain Coaster is one of the few coasters in the region that allows riders to control their speed, offering a customizable ride experience.

Wild Bear Falls Indoor Waterpark

Why You Should Visit: Wild Bear Falls Indoor Waterpark is one of the largest indoor waterparks in the South, offering a range of water attractions including a lazy river, waterslides, and a treehouse play area. The park is climate-controlled, making it a great year-round destination for families.

Website:(https://www.westgateresorts.com/hotels/tennesse e/gatlinburg/westgate-smoky-mountain-resort/wild-bear-falls-water-park/)

Location: 915 Westgate Resorts Rd, Gatlinburg, TN 37738

What to do: Enjoy water slides, a lazy river, and children's play areas.

Packing list: Swimsuits, towels.

Best Time to Visit: Year-round.

Fees: Admission ranges from $15 to $30 depending on age and season.

How to Get There: Located within Westgate Smoky Mountain Resort, accessible by car with parking available.

Closest Town for Accommodation: Westgate Smoky Mountain Resort & Water Park offers comfortable accommodations with full amenities, including the indoor waterpark, dining, and spa services. Location: 915 Westgate Resorts Rd, Gatlinburg, TN 37738, Phone: (865) 430-4800.

GPS Coordinates: 35.7101° N, 83.5300° W

Interesting Facts: The park covers over 60,000 square feet and is themed around the Smoky Mountains, incorporating natural elements into its design.

Gatlinburg Trolley (Gatlinburg)

Why You Should Visit: The Gatlinburg Trolley system offers an affordable and convenient way to explore the city, with routes covering major attractions, shopping areas, and the Great Smoky Mountains National Park. It's a charming and eco-friendly transportation option for tourists.

Website: (https://www.gatlinburgtrolley.org)

Location: Various stops throughout Gatlinburg, TN

What to do: Ride the trolley to explore Gatlinburg's attractions and shopping areas.

Packing list: Comfortable attire and a map of trolley routes.

Best Time to Visit: Year-round; peak tourist seasons may have more frequent service.

Fees: Rides typically cost $1-$2, with unlimited ride passes available.

How to Get There: Accessible from various stops in downtown Gatlinburg.

Closest Town for Accommodation: Clarion Pointe Downtown Gatlinburg offers convenient accommodations, including complimentary breakfast and easy access to trolley stops. Location: 200 East Parkway, Gatlinburg, TN 37738, Phone: (865) 436-5047.

GPS Coordinates: 35.7149° N, 83.5102° W

Interesting Facts: The Gatlinburg Trolley system is one of the largest municipal systems in the U.S., operating 20 trolleys and offering various route options.

Ripley's Haunted Adventure (Gatlinburg)

Why You Should Visit: Ripley's Haunted Adventure is a multi-level haunted house attraction offering a spine-chilling experience with live actors and special effects. It's a popular destination for thrill-seekers and those looking for a spooky adventure in Gatlinburg.

Website: (https://www.ripleys.com/gatlinburg/haunted-adventure/)

Location: 908 Parkway, Gatlinburg, TN 37738

What to do: Experience a haunted house with live actors and special effects.

Packing list: Comfortable attire and sturdy footwear.

Best Time to Visit: Open year-round; evenings for a more atmospheric experience.

Fees: Admission is around $15 for adults.

How to Get There: Located in downtown Gatlinburg, accessible by car with nearby parking.

Closest Town for Accommodation: Greystone Lodge on the River offers cozy accommodations, complimentary breakfast, and proximity to Gatlinburg's main attractions. Location: 559 Parkway, Gatlinburg, TN 37738, Phone: (865) 436-5621.

GPS Coordinates: 35.7121° N, 83.5176° W

Interesting Facts: Ripley's Haunted Adventure is known for its year-round operation, providing a consistent haunted experience even outside the traditional Halloween season.

Northeast Tennessee

Birthplace of Country Music Museum

Why You Should Visit: The Birthplace of Country Music Museum celebrates Bristol's pivotal role in the history of country music, featuring exhibits on the 1927 Bristol Sessions, often called the "Big Bang" of country music. The museum offers interactive exhibits, artifacts, and recordings that highlight the genre's rich heritage and its influence on American music.

Website: (https://www.birthplaceofcountrymusic.org)

Location: 520 Birthplace of Country Music Way, Bristol, VA 24201

What to do: Explore interactive exhibits and learn about the history of country music.

Packing list: Comfortable attire and a camera.

Best Time to Visit: Open year-round.

Fees: General admission is around $13 for adults.

How to Get There: accessible by car with nearby parking.

Closest Town for Accommodation: The Bristol Hotel offers boutique accommodations with modern amenities, located near the museum. Location: 510 Birthplace of Country Music Way, Bristol, VA 24201, Phone: (276) 696-3535.

GPS Coordinates: 36.5951° N, 82.1852° W

Interesting Facts: The museum is an affiliate of the Smithsonian Institution and features a radio station, WBCM-LP, broadcasting live music and interviews.

Bristol Motor Speedway (Bristol)

Why You Should Visit: Bristol Motor Speedway is a legendary NASCAR short track known for its high-banked turns and intense racing action. The speedway hosts major racing events and is a must-visit for motorsports fans. The adjacent Thunder Valley dragstrip adds to the excitement with NHRA drag racing.

Website: (https://www.bristolmotorspeedway.com)

Location: 151 Speedway Blvd, Bristol, TN 37620

What to do: Attend NASCAR and NHRA racing events.

Packing list: Ear protection, comfortable attire, and sunscreen.

Best Time to Visit: Spring and summer for major racing events.

Fees: Ticket prices vary by event.

How to Get There: Accessible by car.

Closest Town for Accommodation: Fairfield Inn & Suites by Marriott Bristol offers comfortable accommodations, complimentary breakfast, and easy access to the speedway. Location: 3285 W State St, Bristol, TN 37620, Phone: (423) 574-4500.

GPS Coordinates: 36.5154° N, 82.2572° W

Interesting Facts: Known as "The Last Great Colosseum," Bristol Motor Speedway can hold up to 153,000 spectators and features a 0.533-mile concrete oval.

South Holston Lake (Bristol)

Why You Should Visit: South Holston Lake is a picturesque reservoir offering a variety of recreational activities, including boating, fishing, swimming, and hiking. The lake's scenic beauty and clear waters make it a popular destination for outdoor enthusiasts and families.

Website: (https://www.tva.com/environment/lake-levels/south-holston)

Location: South Holston Lake, Bristol, TN 37620

What to do: Boating, fishing, swimming, and hiking.

Packing list: Swimsuits, fishing gear, sunscreen, and a picnic.

Best Time to Visit: Late spring to early fall for warm weather and water activities.

Fees: Free entrance; costs may apply for boat rentals.

How to Get There: Accessible by car with various public access points around the lake.

Closest Town for Accommodation: Courtyard by Marriott Bristol offers modern accommodations, a fitness center, and proximity to the lake. Location: 3169 Linden Dr, Bristol, VA 24202, Phone: (276) 591-4400.

GPS Coordinates: 36.5412° N, 82.0948° W

Interesting Facts: The lake is managed by the Tennessee Valley Authority (TVA) and covers over 7,580 acres, offering 168 miles of shoreline.

Steele Creek Park (Bristol)

Why You Should Visit: Steele Creek Park is a large municipal park featuring a beautiful lake, nature trails, a golf course, and a nature center. It offers a range of outdoor activities for visitors of all ages, including paddle boating, fishing, and picnicking.

Website: (https://www.bristoltn.org/151/Steele-Creek-Park)

Location: 4 Little Ln, Bristol, TN 37620

What to do: Paddle boating, fishing, hiking, and picnicking.

Packing list: Comfortable walking shoes, picnic supplies, and a camera.

Best Time to Visit: Spring to fall for nice temperature and outdoor sports.

Fees: Free entrance; fees apply for certain activities like paddle boat rentals.

How to Get There: Accessible by car with ample on-site parking.

Closest Town for Accommodation: Quality Inn & Suites offers comfortable accommodations, complimentary breakfast, and proximity to the park. Location: 3281 W State St, Bristol, TN 37620, Phone: (423) 764-3121.

GPS Coordinates: 36.5647° N, 82.2384° W

Interesting Facts: The park spans over 2,200 acres, making it one of the largest municipal parks in Tennessee, and features a 52-acre lake.

Bristol Caverns (Bristol)

Why You Should Visit: Bristol Caverns offers an exciting underground adventure, with guided tours showcasing stunning rock formations, crystal-clear streams, and expansive chambers. It's a unique natural attraction that provides insight into the geological history of the region.

Website: (https://www.bristolcaverns.com)

Location: 1157 Bristol Caverns Hwy, Bristol, TN 37620

What to do: Take guided tours of the caverns and learn about their formation.

Packing list: Comfortable walking shoes and a light jacket.

Best Time to Visit: Open year-round; ideal for escaping hot or rainy weather.

Fees: Admission is around $20 for adults.

How to Get There: Accessible by car with on-site parking available.

Closest Town for Accommodation: Comfort Inn Bristol offers comfortable rooms, complimentary breakfast, and easy access to the caverns. Location: 2368 Lee Hwy, Bristol, VA 24202, Phone: (276) 466-3881.

GPS Coordinates: 36.5535° N, 82.1418° W

Interesting Facts: The caverns were used by Native Americans as a shelter and later by early settlers for storage and defense.

Viking Hall Civic Center (Bristol)

Why You Should Visit: Viking Hall Civic Center is a versatile event venue hosting concerts, sports events, theater productions, and community gatherings. Its central location and range of events make it a cultural hub for the Bristol community.

Website: (https://www.bristoltn.org/154/Viking-Hall-Civic-Center)

Location: 1100 Edgemont Ave, Bristol, TN 37620

What to do: Attend concerts, theater productions, and community events.

Packing list: Event-appropriate attire and a camera.

Best Time to Visit: Year-round; check the event schedule for specific dates.

Fees: Ticket prices vary by event.

How to Get There: Accessible by car with ample on-site parking.

Closest Town for Accommodation: Econo Lodge Near Motor Speedway offers budget-friendly accommodations, complimentary breakfast, and proximity to the civic center. Location: 912 Commonwealth Ave, Bristol, VA 24201, Phone: (276) 466-2112.

GPS Coordinates: 36.5839° N, 82.1956° W

Interesting Facts: Viking Hall has hosted a variety of notable performances and events, making it a key venue in the region.

Bays Mountain Park & Planetarium

Why You Should Visit: Bays Mountain Park & Planetarium offers over 3,500 acres of nature preserve with hiking trails, a lake, and a state-of-the-art planetarium. It's an ideal destination for outdoor enthusiasts and stargazers, providing educational programs and interactive exhibits.

Website: (https://www.baysmountain.com)

Location: 853 Bays Mountain Park Rd, Kingsport, TN 37660

What to do: Hiking, wildlife viewing, and stargazing at the planetarium.

Packing list: Hiking boots, water, and a camera.

Best Time to Visit: Spring to fall for outdoor activities; year-round for the planetarium.

Fees: Admission is around $5; additional fees for planetarium shows.

How to Get There: Accessible by car with on-site parking available.

Closest Town for Accommodation: MeadowView Marriott Conference Resort & Convention Center offers luxurious accommodations, a golf course, and dining options, located near the park. Location: 1901 Meadowview Pkwy, Kingsport, TN 37660, Phone: (423) 578-6600.

GPS Coordinates: 36.5360° N, 82.5900° W

Interesting Facts: The park's planetarium is one of the largest in Tennessee, offering educational shows and laser light performances.

Warriors' Path State Park (Kingsport)

Why You Should Visit: Warriors' Path State Park is a 950-acre park that offers a wide range of recreational activities including hiking, boating, fishing, golfing, and horseback riding. The park's scenic beauty, along with its well-maintained facilities, makes it a popular destination for outdoor enthusiasts and families.

Website: (https://tnstateparks.com/parks/warriors-path)

Location: 490 Hemlock Rd, Kingsport, TN 37663

What to do: Hiking, boating, fishing, golfing, and horseback riding.

Packing list: Outdoor gear, picnic supplies, and a camera.

Best Time to Visit: Spring to fall for the best weather and outdoor activities.

Fees: Free entrance; fees apply for certain activities like golfing and boat rentals.

How to Get There: Accessible by car with ample on-site parking available.

Closest Town for Accommodation: Comfort Suites Kingsport offers comfortable accommodations, complimentary breakfast, and convenient access to the park. Location: 3005 Bays Meadow Pl, Kingsport, TN 37664, Phone: (423) 765-1955.

GPS Coordinates: 36.4744° N, 82.5011° W

Interesting Facts: The park is named after the Great Indian Warpath, a trail used by Native Americans, and features the popular Fall Creek Loop Trail, which showcases beautiful views of the surrounding landscape.

Exchange Place Living History Farm

Why You Should Visit: Exchange Place Living History Farm is a preserved 19th-century farm that provides a glimpse into the agricultural practices and daily life of the mid-1800s. The farm features historic buildings, heirloom crops, and heritage livestock, offering educational programs and seasonal festivals.

Website: (http://exchangeplace.info)

Location: 4812 Orebank Rd, Kingsport, TN 37664

What to do: Tour historic buildings, attend seasonal festivals, and participate in educational programs.

Packing list: Comfortable walking shoes and a camera.

Best Time to Visit: Spring and fall for seasonal festivals and events.

Fees: Admission fees vary by event; typically around $5 for adults.

How to Get There: Accessible by car with on-site parking available.

Closest Town for Accommodation: Hampton Inn Kingsport offers modern accommodations, complimentary breakfast, and proximity to the farm. Location: 2000 Enterprise Pl, Kingsport, TN 37660, Phone: (423) 247-3888.

GPS Coordinates: 36.5486° N, 82.4892° W

Interesting Facts: Exchange Place was originally a plantation and later became a relay station where horses and riders of the Old Stage Road could exchange their tired mounts for fresh ones.

Kingsport Carousel & Park (Kingsport)

Why You Should Visit: The Kingsport Carousel & Park features a beautiful, hand-carved wooden carousel with 32 animals and two chariots, all crafted by local volunteers. The park also includes a picnic area, playground, and walking trails, making it a delightful spot for families and children.

Website: (https://engagekingsport.com/kingsport-carousel/)

Location: 350 Clinchfield St, Kingsport, TN 37660

What to do: Ride the carousel, enjoy a picnic, and explore the playground and walking trails.

Packing list: Comfortable attire, picnic supplies, and a camera.

Best Time to Visit: Spring to fall for pleasant weather and park activities.

Fees: Carousel rides are typically $1 per ride.

How to Get There: Accessible by car with nearby parking available.

Closest Town for Accommodation: Holiday Inn Express Hotel & Suites Kingsport-Meadowview I-26 offers comfortable rooms, complimentary breakfast, and easy access to the park. Location:

1217 Stewball Cir, Kingsport, TN 37660, Phone: (423) 723-2300.

GPS Coordinates: 36.5461° N, 82.5590° W

Interesting Facts: The Kingsport Carousel is a community project that took over four years to complete, with local artists contributing to the creation of each unique carousel animal.

Central and Southern Tennessee

Jack Daniel's Distillery (Lynchburg)

Why You Should Visit: Jack Daniel's Distillery is the oldest registered distillery in the United States, producing the world-renowned Jack Daniel's Tennessee Whiskey. Visitors can take guided tours to learn about the whiskey-making process, explore the historic distillery grounds, and enjoy whiskey tastings, making it a must-visit for whiskey enthusiasts and history buffs.

Website: (https://www.jackdaniels.com/en-us/visit-us)

Location: 280 Lynchburg Hwy, Lynchburg, TN 37352

What to do: Take guided tours, explore the distillery, and sample whiskey.

Packing list: Comfortable shoes and a camera.

Best Time to Visit: Year-round; spring and fall for pleasant weather.

Fees: Tours range from $15 to $30.

How to Get There: Accessible by car with on-site parking available.

Closest Town for Accommodation: Lynchburg Country Inn offers comfortable accommodations with modern amenities, located near the distillery. Location: 423 Majors Blvd, Lynchburg, TN 37352, Phone: (931) 759-5995.

GPS Coordinates: 35.2830° N, 86.3745° W

Interesting Facts: Despite being located in a dry county where alcohol sales are prohibited, the distillery is allowed to sell its products on-site due to special legislation.

Lynchburg Town Square (Lynchburg)

Why You Should Visit: Lynchburg Town Square is a charming and historic area featuring quaint shops, restaurants, and local businesses. The square is the heart of Lynchburg and offers a glimpse into small-town Tennessee life, making it a perfect spot for a leisurely stroll and exploration.

Website: (https://www.lynchburgtn.com)

Location: Public Square, Lynchburg, TN 37352

What to do: Shop, dine, and explore historic landmarks.

Packing list: Comfortable walking shoes and a camera.

Best Time to Visit: Spring and fall for pleasant weather and local events.

Fees: Free to explore; costs vary by activity and vendor.

How to Get There: Accessible by car with parking available around the square.

Closest Town for Accommodation: Lynchburg Bed & Breakfast offers cozy accommodations with a homely atmosphere, located near the town square. Location: 98

Mechanic St, Lynchburg, TN 37352, Phone: (931) 759-7394.

GPS Coordinates: 35.2833° N, 86.3740° W

Interesting Facts: The town square is home to several historic buildings, including the Moore County Courthouse, and hosts various events and festivals throughout the year.

Moore County Courthouse (Lynchburg)

Why You Should Visit: The Moore County Courthouse is a historic landmark located in the center of Lynchburg Town Square. Built in 1885, the courthouse is known for its beautiful architecture and serves as a symbol of the town's rich history. For those passionate about architecture and history, this is the perfect place.

Website: (https://www.lynchburgtn.com/visiting-lynchburg)

Location: Public Square, Lynchburg, TN 37352

What to do: Explore the historic courthouse and take photos.

Packing list: Camera and comfortable shoes.

Best Time to Visit: Year-round; spring and fall for pleasant weather.

Fees: Free to visit.

How to Get There: Located in the town square, accessible by car with nearby parking.

Closest Town for Accommodation: Lynchburg Country Inn offers comfortable accommodations with modern amenities, located near the courthouse. Location: 423 Majors Blvd, Lynchburg, TN 37352, Phone: (931) 759-5995.

GPS Coordinates: 35.2833° N, 86.3740° W

Interesting Facts: The Moore County Courthouse is listed on the National Register of Historic Places and continues to function as the center of local government.

Lynchburg Hardware & General Store

Why You Should Visit: Lynchburg Hardware & General Store is a historic shop offering Jack Daniel's memorabilia, local crafts, and unique gifts. It's a nostalgic shopping experience that provides visitors with a chance to take home a piece of Lynchburg's history and culture.

Website: (https://www.jackdaniels.com/en-us/visit-us)

Location: 52 Mechanic St N, Lynchburg, TN 37352

What to do: Shop for Jack Daniel's merchandise and local crafts.

Packing list: Shopping bag and comfortable shoes.

Best Time to Visit: Year-round; spring and fall for local events.

Fees: Free to explore; costs vary by purchase.

How to Get There: Located near the distillery and town square, accessible by car with nearby parking.

Closest Town for Accommodation: Lynchburg Bed & Breakfast offers cozy accommodations with a homely atmosphere, located near the store. Location: 98 Mechanic St, Lynchburg, TN 37352, Phone: (931) 759-7394.

GPS Coordinates: 35.2831° N, 86.3744° W

Interesting Facts: The store originally served as a hardware store for the town and has been restored to offer a variety of Jack Daniel's branded products and local goods.

Barrelhouse BBQ (Lynchburg)

Why You Should Visit: Barrelhouse BBQ is a popular local restaurant known for its delicious smoked meats, homemade sauces, and Southern hospitality. It's a must-visit for food lovers looking to experience authentic Tennessee barbecue in a cozy and friendly setting.

Website: (https://www.barrelhousebbq.com)

Location: 105 Mechanic St S, Lynchburg, TN 37352

What to do: Enjoy a meal of smoked meats and Southern sides.

Packing list: Casual attire and a hearty appetite.

Best Time to Visit: Year-round; lunch and dinner hours.

Fees: Meal costs vary; typically $10-$20 per person.

How to Get There: Located near the town square, accessible by car with nearby parking.

Closest Town for Accommodation: Lynchburg Bed & Breakfast offers cozy accommodations with a homely atmosphere, located near the restaurant. Location: 98 Mechanic St, Lynchburg, TN 37352, Phone: (931) 759-7394.

GPS Coordinates: 35.2827° N, 86.3745° W

Interesting Facts: Barrelhouse BBQ has been featured on several food shows and is famous for its "Grilled Cheese on Crack," a unique and popular menu item.

Tennessee Walking Horse Museum

Why You Should Visit: The Tennessee Walking Horse Museum celebrates the history and heritage of the Tennessee Walking Horse, known for its unique gait and gentle nature. The museum features exhibits on the breed's history, famous horses, and the sport of horse showing, making it an interesting stop for equine enthusiasts.

Website: (https://www.twhbea.com)

Location: 27 Main St, Lynchburg, TN 37352

What to do: Explore exhibits on the Tennessee Walking Horse and its history.

Packing list: Comfortable attire and a camera.

Best Time to Visit: Year-round; spring and fall for local events.

Fees: Free admission.

How to Get There: Located in downtown Lynchburg, accessible by car with nearby parking.

Closest Town for Accommodation: Lynchburg Country Inn offers comfortable accommodations with modern amenities, located near the museum. Location: 423 Majors Blvd, Lynchburg, TN 37352, Phone: (931) 759-5995.

GPS Coordinates: 35.2831° N, 86.3740° W

Interesting Facts: The museum is operated by the Tennessee Walking Horse Breeders' and Exhibitors' Association (TWHBEA), dedicated to preserving the legacy of this distinctive breed.

Wiseman Park (Lynchburg)

Why You Should Visit: Wiseman Park is a lovely community park offering recreational facilities, picnic areas, and walking trails. It's a perfect spot for a relaxing afternoon, family gatherings, or enjoying the natural beauty of Lynchburg.

Website: (https://www.lynchburgtn.com)

Location: Main St, Lynchburg, TN 37352

What to do: Enjoy picnicking, walking trails, and outdoor activities.

Packing list: Picnic supplies, comfortable shoes, and a camera.

Best Time to Visit: Spring to fall for pleasant weather.

Fees: Free entrance.

How to Get There: Located in downtown Lynchburg, accessible by car with nearby parking.

Closest Town for Accommodation: Lynchburg Bed & Breakfast offers cozy accommodations with a homely atmosphere, located near the park. Location: 98 Mechanic St, Lynchburg, TN 37352, Phone: (931) 759-7394.

GPS Coordinates: 35.2833° N, 86.3740° W

Interesting Facts: The park is named after a prominent local family and serves as a community hub for events and recreational activities.

Lynchburg Winery (Lynchburg)

Why You Should Visit: Lynchburg Winery offers a selection of locally produced wines, from dry reds to sweet fruit wines. Visitors can enjoy wine tastings, tours, and a relaxing atmosphere in the heart of Lynchburg, making it a delightful stop for wine enthusiasts and those looking to experience local flavors.

Website: (https://www.lynchburgwinery.com)

Location: 34 Hiles St, Lynchburg, TN 37352

What to do: Enjoy wine tastings and tours.

Packing list: Comfortable attire and a camera.

Best Time to Visit: Year-round; afternoons for tastings.

Fees: Tasting fees typically range from $5 to $10.

How to Get There: Located near Lynchburg Town Square, accessible by car with nearby parking.

Closest Town for Accommodation: Lynchburg Bed & Breakfast offers cozy accommodations with a homely atmosphere, located near the winery. Location: 98 Mechanic St, Lynchburg, TN 37352, Phone: (931) 759-7394.

GPS Coordinates: 35.2835° N, 86.3747° W

Interesting Facts: Lynchburg Winery uses local grapes and fruits to produce its wines, offering a true taste of Tennessee.

Diamond Gusset Jeans Store (Lynchburg)

Why You Should Visit: Diamond Gusset Jeans Store is a unique retail destination offering high-quality, American-made jeans. The store features a variety of styles and sizes, known for their comfort and durability, making it a must-visit for those seeking authentic American denim.

Website: (https://www.gusset.com)

Location: 100 Mechanic St S, Lynchburg, TN 37352

What to do: Shop for high-quality jeans and apparel.

Packing list: Comfortable attire and a shopping bag.

Best Time to Visit: Year-round.

Fees: Free to explore; costs vary by purchase.

How to Get There: Located near Lynchburg Town Square, accessible by car with nearby parking.

Closest Town for Accommodation: Lynchburg Bed & Breakfast offers cozy accommodations with a homely atmosphere, located near the store. Location: 98 Mechanic St, Lynchburg, TN 37352, Phone: (931) 759-7394.

GPS Coordinates: 35.2828° N, 86.3745° W

Interesting Facts: Diamond Gusset Jeans are known for their unique gusset design, providing extra comfort and durability.

Lynchburg Cake and Candy Company

Why You Should Visit: Lynchburg Cake and Candy Company offers delicious, locally-made cakes, candies, and chocolates, many of which are infused with Jack Daniel's whiskey. This charming store provides a sweet taste of Lynchburg and makes for a perfect gift or treat.

Website: (https://www.lynchburgcakeandcandy.com)

Location: 353 Friendly Ln, Lynchburg, TN 37352

What to do: Shop for cakes, candies, and chocolates.

Packing list: Casual attire and a sweet tooth.

Best Time to Visit: Year-round; morning or afternoon for the freshest treats.

Fees: Free to explore; costs vary by purchase.

How to Get There: Located near Lynchburg Town Square, accessible by car with nearby parking.

Closest Town for Accommodation: Lynchburg Bed & Breakfast offers cozy accommodations with a homely atmosphere, located near the store. Location: 98 Mechanic St, Lynchburg, TN 37352, Phone: (931) 759-7394.

GPS Coordinates: 35.2841° N, 86.3748° W

Interesting Facts: The Lynchburg Cake and Candy Company is famous for its whiskey-infused treats, offering a unique local flavor that reflects the town's heritage.

Scenic Byways and Natural Wonders

Hiwassee/Ocoee Scenic River State Park

Why You Should Visit: Hiwassee/Ocoee Scenic River State Park offers breathtaking views and thrilling outdoor activities like white-water rafting on the Ocoee River, renowned for its rapids. The park also provides tranquil fishing spots along the Hiwassee River, beautiful hiking trails, and picnic areas, making it a versatile destination for nature lovers.

Website: (https://tnstateparks.com/parks/hiwassee-ocoee)

Location: 404 Spring Creek Rd, Delano, TN 37325

What to do: White-water rafting, fishing, hiking.

Packing list: Water shoes, sunscreen, picnic supplies, and a camera.

Best Time to Visit: Spring to fall.

Fees: Free entrance; costs vary for rafting.

How to Get There: Accessible by car with ample on-site parking available.

Closest Town for Accommodation: Hampton Inn Cleveland offers comfortable accommodations and easy access to the park. Location: 4355 Holiday Inn Express Way NW, Cleveland, TN 37312, Phone: (423) 790-1199.

GPS Coordinates: 35.2322° N, 84.5222° W

Interesting Facts: The Ocoee River hosted the white-water events during the 1996 Atlanta Olympics, making it a premier destination for rafting enthusiasts.

Cherohala Skyway (Tellico Plains)

Why You Should Visit: The Cherohala Skyway is a stunning 43-mile scenic byway that traverses the Cherokee and Nantahala National Forests, offering breathtaking panoramic views, lush forests, and numerous overlooks. It's perfect for a leisurely drive, motorcycle ride, or photography adventure.

Website: (https://www.cherohala.org)

Location: Begins in Tellico Plains, TN, and ends near Robbinsville, NC

What to do: Scenic driving, photography, and picnicking.

Packing list: Camera, snacks, and weather-appropriate clothing.

Best Time to Visit: Fall for vibrant foliage; spring and summer for lush greenery.

Fees: Free to explore.

How to Get There: Accessible by car from Tellico Plains, TN.

Closest Town for Accommodation: Mountain View Cabin Rentals offers rustic cabins with modern amenities, located near the Skyway. Location: 8654 TN-68, Tellico Plains, TN 37385, Phone: (423) 253-2357.

GPS Coordinates: 35.3648° N, 84.2947° W

Interesting Facts: The Cherohala Skyway, completed in 1996, cost about $100 million and took over 30 years to construct, earning the nickname "Skyway to Nowhere" during its development.

Reelfoot Lake State Park (Tiptonville)

Why You Should Visit: Reelfoot Lake State Park is a natural wonder formed by a series of earthquakes in the early 1800s. The park is famous for its birdwatching opportunities, particularly for bald eagles, and offers activities such as fishing, boating, and hiking amidst unique cypress swamps.

Website: (https://tnstateparks.com/parks/reelfoot-lake)

Location: 2595 Highway 21 E, Tiptonville, TN 38079

What to do: Birdwatching, fishing, boating, and hiking.

Packing list: Binoculars, fishing gear, comfortable shoes, and a camera.

Best Time to Visit: Spring and fall for birdwatching and pleasant weather.

Fees: Free entrance; fees apply for boat rentals and guided tours.

How to Get There: Accessible by car with on-site parking available.

Closest Town for Accommodation: Reelfoot Lake Inn offers comfortable accommodations with lake views and easy access to park activities. Location: 1520 State Route 21 E, Tiptonville, TN 38079, Phone: (731) 253-6845.

GPS Coordinates: 36.3657° N, 89.4142° W

Interesting Facts: Reelfoot Lake is known as the "Earthquake Lake" and is one of the only naturally occurring large lakes in Tennessee, offering unique ecological and geological features.

Discovery Park of America (Union City)

Why You Should Visit: Discovery Park of America is a sprawling museum and heritage park that combines science, history, art, and technology through interactive exhibits and engaging displays. The park includes a 50-acre heritage park, a giant human maze, and numerous indoor and outdoor exhibits.

Website: (https://www.discoveryparkofamerica.com)

Location: 830 Everett Blvd, Union City, TN 38261

What to do: Explore interactive exhibits, heritage park, and special events.

Packing list: Comfortable walking shoes, camera, and weather-appropriate clothing.

Best Time to Visit: Year-round; check the website for special events.

Fees: Admission ranges from $10 to $15.

How to Get There: Accessible by car with ample on-site parking available.

Closest Town for Accommodation: Hampton Inn Union City offers modern amenities and is conveniently located near Discovery Park. Location: 2201 W Reelfoot Ave, Union City, TN 38261, Phone: (731) 885-8850.

GPS Coordinates: 36.4265° N, 89.0584° W

Interesting Facts: Discovery Park of America was founded by Robert and Jenny Kirkland to provide educational and recreational opportunities to the region.

The Cotton Museum (Memphis)

Why You Should Visit: The Cotton Museum in Memphis explores the history and significance of the cotton industry in the American South. It features exhibits on the economic, cultural, and social impact of cotton, making it an essential visit for history enthusiasts and those interested in Southern heritage.

Website: (https://www.memphiscottonmuseum.org)

Location: 65 Union Ave, Memphis, TN 38103

What to do: Explore historical exhibits, watch educational films, and learn about the cotton industry.

Packing list: Comfortable attire and a camera.

Best Time to Visit: Year-round.

Fees: Admission is around $10 for adults.

How to Get There: Located in downtown Memphis, accessible by car or public transportation.

Closest Town for Accommodation: The Peabody Memphis offers luxurious accommodations and is located near the museum. Location: 149 Union Ave, Memphis, TN 38103, Phone: (901) 529-4000.

GPS Coordinates: 35.1426° N, 90.0520° W

Interesting Facts: The Cotton Museum is housed in the historic Memphis Cotton Exchange Building, which played a central role in the global cotton market.

Dyer County Historical Museum

Why You Should Visit: The Dyer County Historical Museum offers an in-depth look into the local history of Dyer County, featuring artifacts, photographs, and exhibits that showcase the area's heritage. It's an excellent stop for those interested in local history and genealogy.

Website: No dedicated website available.

Location: 1015 E Court St, Dyersburg, TN 38024

What to do: Explore historical exhibits and learn about local history.

Packing list: Comfortable attire and a camera.

Best Time to Visit: Year-round; check local listings for opening hours.

Fees: Free admission; donations appreciated.

How to Get There: Accessible by car with on-site parking available.

Closest Town for Accommodation: Sleep Inn & Suites Dyersburg I-155 offers comfortable accommodations and modern amenities, located near the museum. Location: 824 Reelfoot Dr, Dyersburg, TN 38024, Phone: (731) 287-0248.

GPS Coordinates: 36.0342° N, 89.3848° W

Interesting Facts: The museum is located in a historic building that once served as the county jail, adding to its unique charm.

Hatchie National Wildlife Refuge

Why You Should Visit: Hatchie National Wildlife Refuge is a haven for birdwatchers and nature enthusiasts, offering over 11,000 acres of protected wetlands, forests, and streams. The refuge is home to a diverse array of wildlife, including migratory birds, making it an excellent destination for outdoor recreation and wildlife photography.

Website: (https://www.fws.gov/refuge/hatchie)

Location: 6772 Highway 76 S, Brownsville, TN 38012

What to do: Birdwatching, wildlife photography, and hiking.

Packing list: Binoculars, camera, and comfortable walking shoes.

Best Time to Visit: Spring and fall for bird migration seasons.

Fees: Free entrance.

How to Get There: Accessible by car with ample on-site parking available.

Closest Town for Accommodation: Comfort Inn Brownsville offers comfortable accommodations and modern amenities, located near the refuge. Location: 120 Sunny Hill Cove, Brownsville, TN 38012, Phone: (731) 772-4082.

GPS Coordinates: 35.5750° N, 89.2844° W

Interesting Facts: The refuge is part of the larger Hatchie River watershed, one of the most ecologically significant areas in the southeastern United States.

Alex Haley House and Museum

Why You Should Visit: The Alex Haley House and Museum is the childhood home of Alex Haley, the renowned author of "Roots." The museum offers a deep dive into Haley's life and works, as well as the broader history of African Americans in Tennessee. It features exhibits, memorabilia, and guided tours that provide a rich educational experience.

Website: (https://www.tnstateparks.com/parks/alex-haley-museum-and-interpretive-center)

Location: 200 S Church St, Henning, TN 38041

What to do: Explore exhibits on Alex Haley's life and African American history.

Packing list: Comfortable walking shoes and a camera.

Best Time to Visit: Year-round.

Fees: Admission is around $5 for adults.

How to Get There: Accessible by car with on-site parking available.

Closest Town for Accommodation: Sleep Inn & Suites Brownsville offers modern amenities and easy access to the museum. Location: 111 Hospital Dr, Brownsville, TN 38012, Phone: (731) 772-7711.

GPS Coordinates: 35.6754° N, 89.5739° W

Interesting Facts: Alex Haley's "Roots" won a Pulitzer Prize and has been adapted into a popular TV miniseries, bringing the history of African Americans to a broad audience.

Shiloh National Military Park (Shiloh)

Why You Should Visit: Shiloh National Military Park preserves the site of the Battle of Shiloh, one of the major early battles in the American Civil War. The park offers historical monuments, preserved battlefields, a visitor center with exhibits, and interpretive programs, making it a significant destination for history enthusiasts.

Website: (https://www.nps.gov/shil/index.htm)

Location: 1055 Pittsburg Landing Rd, Shiloh, TN 38376

What to do: Tour the battlefields, visit historical monuments, and explore the museum.

Packing list: Comfortable walking shoes, sunscreen, and a camera.

Best Time to Visit: Spring and fall for pleasant weather and outdoor exploration.

Fees: Free entrance.

How to Get There: Accessible by car with on-site parking available.

Closest Town for Accommodation: Hampton Inn Corinth offers modern amenities and is located near the park. Location: 2107 US-72, Corinth, MS 38834, Phone: (662) 286-5949.

GPS Coordinates: 35.1517° N, 88.3251° W

Interesting Facts: The Battle of Shiloh resulted in nearly 24,000 casualties, making it one of the bloodiest battles in the Civil War, and significantly impacting the course of the war.

Fall Creek Falls State Park (Spencer)

Why You Should Visit: Fall Creek Falls State Park is one of Tennessee's largest and most visited state parks, known for its stunning waterfalls, including the 256-foot Fall Creek Falls. The park offers a variety of outdoor activities such as hiking, camping, fishing, and birdwatching, set amidst beautiful natural scenery.

Website: (https://tnstateparks.com/parks/fall-creek-falls)

Location: 2009 Village Camp Rd, Spencer, TN 38585

What to do: Hiking, camping, fishing, and birdwatching.

Packing list: Hiking boots, camping gear, and a camera.

Best Time to Visit: For the greatest weather and beauty, visit in the spring or fall.

Fees: Free entrance; fees apply for camping and certain activities.

How to Get There: Accessible by car with on-site parking available.

Closest Town for Accommodation: The Way Inn offers cozy accommodations with modern amenities, located near the park. Location: 3003 Old Spencer Rd, Spencer, TN 38585, Phone: (931) 946-2111.

GPS Coordinates: 35.6612° N, 85.3562° W

Interesting Facts: Fall Creek Falls is one of the highest free-fall waterfalls in the eastern United States, making it a highlight of the park's natural attractions.

MAPS SECTION

Navigating with QR Codes

To elevate your travel experience, we've integrated a special QR code map that brings all of key attractions into one user-friendly format.

Here's how you can maximize this feature:

1. Discover the QR Code: Within this guide, you'll find a QR code that unlocks all the essential details for exploring Virginia's top attractions.

2. Effortless Scanning:

- Open your smartphone's camera app.

- Point the camera at the QR code.

- Tap the notification that appears to access the link.

3. Interactive Exploration: Upon scanning, you'll be directed to a dynamic digital map. This map allows you to:

- Zoom in and out detailed views.

- Click on for various attractions to access comprehensive information.

4. Seamless Navigation: Utilize the map to obtain directions and navigate to each destination. The map may also feature:

- Reviews from other travelers.

- Stunning photos to preview the sights.

- Insider tips to enhance your visit.

By leveraging this QR code map, you can effortlessly discover and reach must-see attractions. This tool ensures a smooth and enriching travel journey, making every moment of your exploration enjoyable and memorable.

Viewing the Interactive Map with the link

To help you navigate through the attractions with ease, we've provided an interactive map accessible via the link in this guide.

Below here's the link and how you can use it:

https://www.google.com/maps/d/edit?mid=16A7yqWNnoy pA69w-aJqIMc9-UbLp2BE&usp=sharing

1. Access the Link: If you're reading this guide on a digital device, simply click on the link.

If you have a printed version, type the URL into the web browser of your smartphone or computer.

2. Explore the Interactive Map: The link will take you directly to our interactive map.

To obtain a better perspective of the region, you can zoom in and out.

Click on various attractions to get detailed information, including descriptions, photos, and reviews.

3. Navigate the Attractions: Use the map to plan your route and get directions to each attraction.

The interactive map will help you explore the area efficiently and ensure you don't miss any must-see spots

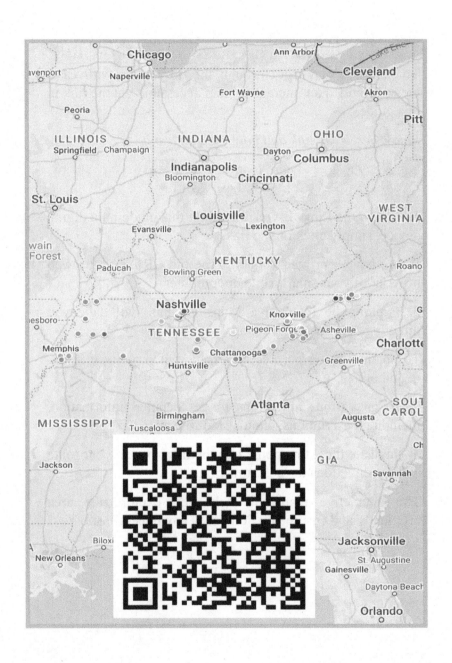

131

Conclusion

As you finish your journey through Tennessee, you'll see why this state is so special. From the misty mountains in the east to the mighty Mississippi River in the west, Tennessee offers a little bit of everything.

Remember, the real magic of Tennessee isn't just in its famous spots. It's in the friendly smiles of the locals, the taste of hot chicken in Nashville, or the peaceful feeling of watching the sun set over the Smoky Mountains.

This guide is just the start. Tennessee has many more secrets waiting for you to find. Maybe you'll discover a hidden waterfall, a cozy small-town diner, or a street musician who plays your new favorite song.

Whether you checked off every item on this bucket list or just a few, you've now got a piece of Tennessee in your heart. The state's motto is "America at its best," and after your visit, you might just agree.

So pack your bags, bring your sense of adventure, and get ready to make some unforgettable memories. Tennessee welcomes you back anytime – there's always more to explore in the Volunteer State!

Made in the USA
Monee, IL
25 November 2024

71244557R00075